RENEWALS 458-4574
DATE DUE

Transfer Pricing Audits in China

Also by same authors

INTERNATIONAL TRANSFER PRICING

Transfer Pricing Audits in China

Jian Li and Alan Paisey

© Jian Li and Alan Paisey 2007

All rights reserved. No reproduction, copy or transmission of this publication may be made without written permission.

No paragraph of this publication may be reproduced, copied or transmitted save with written permission or in accordance with the provisions of the Copyright, Designs and Patents Act 1988, or under the terms of any licence permitting limited copying issued by the Copyright Licensing Agency, 90 Tottenham Court Road, London W1T 4LP.

Any person who does any unauthorized act in relation to this publication may be liable to criminal prosecution and civil claims for damages.

The authors have asserted their rights to be identified as the authors of this work in accordance with the Copyright, Designs and Patents Act 1988.

First published 2007 by
PALGRAVE MACMILLAN
Houndmills, Basingstoke, Hampshire RG21 6XS and
175 Fifth Avenue, New York, N.Y. 10010
Companies and representatives throughout the world

PALGRAVE MACMILLAN is the global academic imprint of the Palgrave Macmillan division of St. Martin's Press, LLC and of Palgrave Macmillan Ltd. Macmillan® is a registered trademark in the United States, United Kingdom and other countries. Palgrave is a registered trademark in the European Union and other countries.

ISBN 13: 978–0–230–00196–1   hardback
ISBN 10: 0–230–00196–3   hardback

This book is printed on paper suitable for recycling and made from fully managed and sustained forest sources.

A catalogue record for this book is available from the British Library.

Library of Congress Cataloging-in-Publication Data

Li, Jian, 1967 Feb. 25–
  Transfer pricing audits in China / Jian Li and Alan Paisey.
    p. cm.
  Includes bibliographical references and index.
  ISBN-13: 978–0–230–00196–1
  ISBN-10: 0–230–00196–3
  1. Transfer pricing–China. 2. International business enterprises–Taxation–China. 3. International business enterprises–China–Auditing. I. Paisey, Alan. II. Title.

HD62.45.L53 2007
658.8'160951–dc22   2006050505

10 9 8 7 6 5 4 3 2 1
16 15 14 13 12 11 10 09 08 07

Printed and bound in Great Britain by
Antony Rowe Ltd, Chippenham and Eastbourne

Contents

List of Figures	viii
List of Tables	ix
Preface	xii
Foreword	xiv

Part I Field of Audit — 1

Chapter 1 Foreign Direct Investments and Enterprises — 3

Introduction	3
Theories of foreign direct investment	4
Trends and patterns in China	7
Foreign direct investment and foreign trade	14
Summary	17

Chapter 2 Transfer Pricing in Concept — 18

Introduction	18
Company international tax planning	18
Multinational tax management perspective	21
Chinese practice	26
Summary	30

Part II Mechanics of Audit — 31

Chapter 3 Transfer Pricing Rules of Trading Partners — 33

Introduction	33
Transfer pricing methods	34
OECD transfer pricing guidelines	35
United States	37
Canada	39
France	40
Germany	41
Italy	42
Japan	43
United Kingdom	43
Summary	44

Chapter 4 China's Transfer Pricing Rules   45

Introduction   45
Current transfer pricing rules   46
China's transfer pricing regime   48
Summary   51

Chapter 5 Associated Enterprises   56

Introduction   56
Organizational structure   56
Related party identity   61
Related party transactions   64
Summary   68

Chapter 6 Audit Adjustment Methods   69

Introduction   69
Arm's length principle   69
Transfer pricing methods   71
Selecting the transfer pricing method   78
Double taxation and competent authority   79
Summary   81

Chapter 7 Documentation and Penalties   83

Introduction   83
Current requirements   83
Maintenance of documentation   85
Functional analysis   86
Cost sharing agreement   88
Fines and charges   89
Summary   89

Chapter 8 Advance Pricing Agreements   90

Introduction   90
Case in point   90
Applying for an advance pricing agreement   92
Summary   99

Chapter 9 Contemporary Audit System   101

Introduction   101
Tax audit procedures   101
Tax audit structure and practice   108
Operational data   108
Summary   111

Part III Experience of Audit — 113

Chapter 10 Foreign Company Practice — 115
Introduction — 115
Company data — 115
Transfer pricing methods used — 119
Factors affecting transfer pricing — 120
Organizational and environmental variable rankings — 126
Statistical references — 127
Summary — 133

Chapter 11 Audit in Action — 134
Introduction — 134
Cases of transfer pricing audits — 134
Tangible goods — 134
Intangible goods — 142
Services — 144
Finance — 144
Summary — 145

Chapter 12 Audit Risk Levels — 149
Introduction — 149
Personal perspectives of tax officials — 149
Tax authority perspectives — 151
Audit risk model — 153
Audit policy and practice development — 157
Summary — 159

Chapter 13 Managing the Audit — 160
Introduction — 160
Tax authorities at work — 160
Personal viewpoint — 166
Summary — 169

Chapter 14 Audits in Future — 170
Introduction — 170
Development markers — 170
Managing audit risks — 172
In conclusion — 177

Bibliography — 178

Index — 181

List of Figures

2.1	Transfer pricing model for two company units located in different countries	22
2.2	Transfer pricing with a tax haven for tax planning purposes	24
5.1	A single focus business model	57
5.2	A divisionalized multi-product business model	58
5.3	A vertically integrated business model	60
5.4	A conglomerate multinational enterprise model	61
5.5	Indirectly related party transactions	63
5.6	Intercompany transaction of tangible assets	65
5.7	Intercompany transaction of intangible assets	66
5.8	Transfer pricing in a pharmaceutical group	66
5.9	Intercompany transaction of services	67
5.10	Intercompany transaction of financing	68
6.1	The arm's length principle	70
6.2	Comparable uncontrolled price method model	73
6.3	Resale price method model	73
6.4	Cost plus method model	74
6.5	Profit split method model	76
6.6	Comparable profit method model	77
8.1	A bilateral advance pricing agreement model	92
9.1	Steps in the procedure for conducting a transfer pricing audit	112
10.1	Transaction flows for a motor car company	132
11.1	Transaction flows for Audit Case 5	137
11.2	Transaction flows for Audit Case 14	143
13.1	Transaction flows for the exemplary audit case	169

List of Tables

1.1	Foreign direct investment in China, 1990–2004	8
1.2	Forms of foreign direct investment to December 2004 (US$ billion)	9
1.3	Foreign direct investment from the top ten countries to December 2004 (US$ billion)	10
1.4	Regional distribution of actual foreign direct investment to December 2004	10
1.5	The provincial distribution of actual foreign direct investment by the top 500 multinationals in 2002	12
1.6	Distribution of actual foreign direct investment to December 2003 according to industry (US$ 100 million)	13
1.7	Distribution of actual foreign direct investment by the top 500 multinationals in China in 2002 according to industry	14
1.8	Portions of China's total exports and imports contributed by foreign investment enterprises (FIEs) 1990–2004 (US$ billion)	15
1.9	Exports by foreign investment enterprises to the main countries or other destinations, 1991–1994 (US$ 100 million)	16
1.10	Imports by foreign investment enterprises from the main countries or other sources, 1991–1994 (US$ 100 million)	16
2.1	Market price versus manipulated transfer price	23
2.2	Income tax rates of some of China's main trading partners	27
3.1	Acceptable transfer pricing methods	36
4.1	Tax authority and tax law	51
4.2	Regulations, rules and guidelines	52
4.3	Acceptable methods	53
4.4	Priorities of methods	53
4.5	Transfer pricing penalties	53
4.6	Reductions in penalties	54
4.7	Documentation requirements	54
4.8	Return disclosures/related party disclosures	55
4.9	Advance pricing agreements available	55

5.1	Relationship tests as defined in the transfer pricing regulations of China and other main industrial countries	63
6.1	Functional analysis for a profit split method audit for the case in Figure 6.5	76
6.2	Characteristics of the transfer pricing methods used for audits	79
6.3	Profit adjustment and double taxation (US$)	80
7.1	Advised quality levels of processes and documentation for dealings with foreign associated enterprises	84
8.1	Advantages and disadvantages of an advance pricing agreement	98
9.1	Return for foreign investment enterprises concerning business dealings with associated companies – Type A Form	103
9.2	Return for foreign investment enterprises concerning business dealings with associated companies – Type B Form	103
10.1	The home country/region of the companies surveyed	116
10.2	Intercompany transfers as percentages of total company transfers	116
10.3	The nature and frequency of intercompany transfers of tangible goods, intangible goods, services, and finances	116
10.4	The legally oriented transfer pricing methods used in order of frequency	117
10.5	Transfer pricing methods used in practice according to industry in order of frequency	118
10.6	Transfer pricing methods used by the respondent firms of different nationalities in order of frequency	118
10.7	Transfer pricing methods used by the respondent companies	119
10.8	Reported transfer pricing tax audits	120
10.9	Rankings of the importance of the organizational and environmental variables for transfer pricing policy decisions by respondent firms of different nationalities	126
10.10	Logistic regression analysis of the significance of the organizational and environmental variables	129
10.11	Home country of the subsidiary respondent firms that are currently using or considering advance pricing agreements (APA)	131
11.1	Summary of audit cases	146

12.1	Company features most likely to encourage transfer pricing abuses as cited by tax authorities	152
12.2	Methods used by tax authorities to calculate true liabilities and tax payment adjustments in cases of transfer pricing abuse	153
12.3	Company performance variables affecting audit risk levels	155
14.1	Anticipated changes in trading conditions in China	174

Preface

Following the publication of *International Transfer Pricing in Asia Pacific* (2005), it seemed that a logical step should be taken to focus on the interaction between the company and the tax authority with regard to transfer pricing practice in China. Having mentioned in that book the existence of the audit as a means to deter companies from malpractice and to redress the tax losses suffered by the Chinese government as a result of them, a natural corollary was to explore the audit itself.

Consequently, this book presents an introduction and overview of the audit in China as specifically directed at transfer pricing abuse. Primarily intended as it is for people directly involved in, and associated with, business activities in and connected with China, it covers the practical dimensions of the subject, the 14 chapters being subdivided for the convenience of the reader into three parts.

Part I, consisting of Chapters 1–2, provides a background on foreign investment in China and the transfer pricing to which it gives rise. Part II, covering Chapters 3–9, overviews the way in which the audit operates, with the basis and principles on which it works. Part III, including Chapters 10–14, presents the audit as an experience by both the company and the tax authority, concluding with an attempt to mark the path of the future for audit in China.

The subject as a whole lies at the heart of confidentiality and secrecy, according to formal statute, cultural propensities, and business practice in China. The constraints that would normally make this study difficult to access by an outsider have been mitigated by the generosity of contacted Chinese tax authority officials, who cannot be named but to whom we extend our grateful thanks.

Although China in general, and its economic institutions in particular, are not yet used to the interchanges with independent enquiry to anything like the extent that exists in the European and American Continents, it appears that the former endemic reluctance and suspicion in Chinese public circles has given way a little to an interest in, and willingness to respond to, research enquiry. Since government institutions – as part of the full spectrum of a nation's institutions – in all countries are least open to such enquiry, we have been doubly fortunate in being able to obtain data from the inside of the audit estate itself.

In having had access to computer technical advice from Sheila Smurthwaite for the preparation of this book, we wish to thank her for her assistance during the work on it.

Jian Li and Alan Paisey
Australia and New Zealand
August 2006

Foreword

Susan C. Borkowski, Ph. D. Lindback Professor of Accounting and Joint Faculty Integrated Science Business Technology Program, La Salle University, Philadelphia PA, USA.

> No longer an obscure concern of a few corporate giants, transfer pricing is now considered to be the most significant international tax issue for executives of multinational companies.
>
> Kral, 2005

In survey after survey conducted during the past decade, transfer pricing is consistently identified as the most important tax issue facing transnational corporations (TNCs), now and in the foreseeable future. The next most important issues identified are tax minimization and double taxation, both of which are directly correlated with a TNC's transfer pricing strategy.

Unfortunately, there is something of a disconnection today between the importance of transfer pricing practices for TNCs and the academic analyses of their transfer pricing activities. In a 2005 survey of the world's largest TNCs by the accounting firm Ernst & Young, executives from the participating TNCs overwhelmingly identified transfer pricing as the most significant tax issue facing their companies now and in the immediate future. However, there is a definite deficiency in the number, depth, and breadth of research studies on 1) the transfer pricing strategies and practices of TNCs, and 2) the results of those strategies and practices *vis-à-vis* a TNC's audit status with various tax authorities. The urgency exhibited by TNC executives regarding transfer pricing issues is not yet reflected in current academic research, as evidenced by the trickle of published studies in the subject field.

So, to start at the beginning, what exactly is transfer pricing, and why is it so crucial to TNC managers? Transfer pricing is an international tax strategy used by corporations with cross-border transactions to maximize profits while simultaneously minimizing tax liabilities in the countries in which they have a presence. This presence can be manifested through a subsidiary, division, affiliate, or other organizational unit in one or more host countries, each with its own tax authority and its own transfer pricing regulations. The most tax-efficient transfer pricing strategy implemented by a TNC involves assigning prices to the tangible products, intangible assets, and services transferred across borders by the parent TNC to its related entities, and *vice versa*. The TNC must simultaneously ensure that this transfer pricing activity is adhering to the complex transfer pricing regulations administered by the tax authorities of each of the countries concerned.

If transfer pricing is considered by TNCs and academics as an international tax strategy, why do the tax authorities of most developed and developing countries need to have detailed transfer pricing legislation and regulations in place? Transfer pricing allows a TNC to minimize its tax liabilities by shifting profits across borders, so that more of its profits are recognized in tax jurisdictions with lower corporate tax rates, such as Ireland. This effectively reduces the tax revenues in the tax jurisdictions with higher corporate tax rates, such as the United States. It is this reduction in the inflow of tax revenues from TNCs doing business in their country that immediately gets the attention of a country's tax authority.

The goals of TNCs that have strategically implemented transfer pricing policies are diametrically opposed to the goals of a country's tax authority. The goals of the latter are to assess and collect the appropriate taxes that arise from a TNC's domestic and cross-border transactions, given the framework of that country's transfer pricing regulations. In other words, the tax authorities want to maximize the collection of tax revenues while minimizing the taxes lost due to the transfer pricing strategies employed by TNCs operating in their countries.

So, why a book about transfer pricing audits, particularly as they relate to China? First, it is in order to have some understanding of the current global audit environment. In the 2005 Ernst & Young survey, 65% of the TNCs in the sample had experienced an audit triggered by their transfer pricing strategies. Of those audits, 40% resulted in an adjustment to the TNC's tax liabilities. Why was there such a high audit percentage? Why are audits triggered by a TNC's transfer pricing transactions?

If 65% of TNCs are audited as a result of their transfer pricing activity, are tax authorities out of control? A measured answer to this question is no, tax authorities are not out of control. This audit percentage simply reflects the current transfer pricing regulatory environment. This percentage is certainly high relative to the audit status of TNCs

15 years ago. In the early 1990s, the United States was the only country that aggressively enforced its transfer pricing regulations and audited TNCs that were suspected of not being in compliance. Australia soon followed suit.

If we fast-forward 15 years to 2006, about 50 countries have joined Australia and the United States in implementing and enforcing transfer pricing regulations. Many tax authorities also have detailed penalties in force if a TNC fails to keep adequate documentation of its transfer pricing transactions. There are also severe penalties if a TNC shifts profits excessively, such that the taxes paid by the TNC are significantly understated.

The tax authorities of many countries are actively scrutinizing the transfer pricing activity of both home country TNCs and host country TNCs to ensure compliance with existing transfer pricing regulations, and, in cases of non-compliance, imposing penalties ranging from nuisance amounts to significant assessments in cases of deliberate transfer pricing manipulation to shift profits, and artificially minimize tax liabilities in violation of the regulations.

In her study of the policy implications of cross-border tax arbitrage, Diane Ring identifies the central challenge in international tax as navigating the relationship between an individual country's tax system and the rest of the world. Her thesis is that the dilemma for developed and developing countries is how to balance the competing demands of revenue, domestic policy, retaliation, and global goals. The dilemma becomes more urgent and fraught with danger as the pace of interactions among tax regimes escalates in response to the increasing global reach of TNCs.

This concern with using transfer pricing strategies to shift profits and minimize taxes is not a new development. More than 25 years ago, the Pacific Association of Tax Administrators was formed in response to the increased use of tax havens by TNCs to evade taxes. The countries comprising the intergovernmental tax group, hereafter called PATA, are Australia, Canada, Japan, and the United States. In its first meeting, held in Hawaii in 1981, its mission was to discuss the various tax evasion techniques, particularly transfer pricing.

PATA issued its first, long-awaited uniform transfer pricing documentation package in 2003. If a TNC prepares its transfer pricing documentation according to its principles, this package will satisfy the documentation requirements of the tax authorities in the four member countries of PATA. This theoretically lessens the workload of TNCs while providing them with the assurance that penalties will not be assessed. There are 53 requirements that a TNC must satisfy, making the package more stringent than the previously existing documentation requirements of each of the four countries. However, if the resulting documentation package does satisfy multiple tax authorities, the work required should still be less than that needed to create individual documentation packages for each tax authority in turn.

To reduce the time, money, and energy spent on transfer pricing audits by both the tax authorities and the TNCs, and to combat aggressive profit-shifting behaviour by an increasing number of TNCs, advance pricing agreements (APA) were created. An APA allows a TNC and a tax authority to come to an agreement about what transfer pricing methods are deemed acceptable, given existing transfer pricing regulations, and guarantees the acceptability of the given transfer pricing method for a multi-year period.

In 2004, PATA members agreed to encourage the use of bilateral APAs by TNCs, and drew up common procedures on how the competent authority parts of bilateral APAs should be handled. PATA hoped that its bilateral advance pricing arrangement (BAPA) guidance will simplify the process and cut down the time and effort currently required to complete an APA. However, even with this detailed guidance, conflicts among the tax authorities of the four member countries are developing, particularly between the tax authority of the United States (the Internal Revenue Service) and the tax authorities of both Canada (Revenue Canada) and Japan (National Tax Agency). These tax authorities are critical of each other's attempts to claim TNCs' profits and associated tax revenues for themselves, at the expense of each other's tax revenues.

In 2004, PATA also issued its guidance for TNCs that were seeking mutual agreement procedures (MAP) to settle cross-border and double taxation issues in a timely, consistent and transparent manner. MAPs offer an alternative venue for TNCs to settle double taxation issues arising from cross-border transfer pricing activities. The common objective of both the BAPA and MAP guidance is to improve upon existing levels of transparency in the processes connected with the transfer pricing activities of TNCs. While the documentation packages and operational guidance in concept are steps forward, they are voluntary and affect only the four PATA nations. The hope is that other countries, while not officially part of PATA, will see the value of, and will adopt, the various packages it has produced to date.

So, where does China fit in? Considered by many to be the world's largest and most important untapped market opportunity, many non-Chinese TNCs are looking to share in that opportunity. The Chinese market exceeds 1.3 billion people (roughly 20% of the world's population). China is among the world's fastest developing economies. It is becoming increasingly attractive as a host country due to its improved infrastructure and the modernization of its capital markets. Its exports in 2005 have been estimated at US$ 760–800 billion. What company would, or could refuse to chase after an entrée to such a market? The 2005 Ernst & Young transfer pricing survey reported that 35% of TNCs identified China as a current beneficiary of their manufacturing investment. China is also the recipient of increasing amounts of foreign research and development (R&D) investment. Of these investments into China, 42% of the manufacturing investment, and 84% of the R&D investment came from TNCs based in the Americas.

Another recent survey conducted by PricewaterhouseCoopers (2006) revealed the downside for TNCs doing business in Asia Pacific countries. China (with India in a distant second place) was identified by the respondent TNCs as the country presenting the greatest tax challenges to them in the 21st century. Some of the reasons cited were the lack of established transfer pricing regulations, the differing interpretations of those regulations by different Chinese officials, language issues, and cultural obstacles. As non-Chinese TNCs negotiate with the Chinese government to establish subsidiaries in China, they also face the issue of transfer pricing so that they may be able properly to allocate profits and tax revenues to both China and their home countries.

Although very new to the transfer pricing arena, the Chinese tax authority, the State Administration of Taxation (SAT) is astute. It has quickly adapted its outlook to the transnational cross-border business model and is becoming a force that should not be underestimated by TNCs, nor by the tax authorities of other countries. Given the current rate of transfer pricing related regulations and guidance from the SAT, China may soon have the most comprehensive transfer pricing program in the Asia-Pacific region, surpassing even that of Japan, which administers one of the world's most well-established transfer pricing regimes. The year 2004 saw the SAT release its revamped transfer pricing regulations that are now in effect. These regulations mirror those already in place in many other countries that have older, more established transfer pricing regimes, and bolster the findings of a recent PricewaterhouseCoopers survey which found that 94% of TNCs identified Asia as their highest risk area regarding transfer pricing.

Chinese regulations describe the acceptable methods for determining the transfer price of tangible goods. They include comparable uncontrolled price, resale price, cost-plus, and other reasonable methods, including the transactional net margin, and the profit split methods. While these regulations are very impressive on paper, there is an overriding concern about how difficult it may be for TNCs to adhere to these regulations, and for the SAT fairly and consistently to enforce these regulations. For example, finding comparable companies in China to establish the comparable uncontrolled price for a product is currently, and will remain, difficult for TNCs for the foreseeable future, due to the relative paucity of publicly available and/or published data about Chinese companies, as well as the relatively small size of the majority of Chinese companies when compared with their non-Chinese TNC counterparts.

Documentation rules from the SAT are expected by the end of 2006, as is guidance regarding cost sharing arrangements. The SAT has quickly adopted the APA concept, and, as of June 2006, has negotiated its first bilateral advance pricing arrangement with Japan. At the same time, the SAT has charged that many foreign-based TNCs are shifting profits out of China, or are significantly underreporting the profits that should be taxed in China. Thus, the SAT is more aggressively enforcing its transfer pricing regulations, particularly as they apply to foreign TNCs in general, and to Japan in particular. The SAT is particularly interested in auditing TNCs which consistently report losses. Chinese transfer pricing adjustments to foreign-based TNC profits doubled from 2000 to 2004, and are continuing to increase.

Transfer pricing audits in China have a critical dimension that is missing or much less in evidence in audits undertaken by tax authorities in most other countries. The Asian culture in general, and the Chinese culture and values in particular, stress respect and collaboration. Thus, non-Asian-based TNCs will find themselves necessarily reinventing their approach to transfer pricing audits if they hope to have a favourable outcome. For example, a TNC based in the United States entering into an audit meeting with the IRS typically approaches it very forcefully with an intent to win, by adopting an 'the end justifies the means' philosophy. The SAT would view this approach as aggressive, impersonal, and excitable. In China, this attitude would almost guarantee an unfavourable outcome to the audit. This is because an aggressive, no-holds-barred, confrontational, and impersonal approach by the TNC (considered rude at best by Chinese standards), would embarrass the Chinese SAT officials and cause them to 'lose face', a serious breach of cultural etiquette in China. This approach could also cause the SAT officials to lose composure during the meeting, precipitating yet another serious breach of Chinese etiquette.

Therefore, not only do foreign-based TNCs need to be well-versed in the rapidly changing world of Chinese transfer pricing regulations, they also need to understand the Chinese culture and the ramifications of behaviour not considered acceptable within that culture. Chinese culture dictates that the SAT must not openly reject the TNC's position and should avoid open conflict whenever possible in order to 'save the TNC's face'.

Coupled with the fact that the SAT does not have any guidelines for how quickly an audit should be concluded, an audit could indeed stretch out over several years, if the TNC is unwilling to agree with even part of the SAT's assessment. Again, an unwillingness to compromise on the part of the TNC causes the SAT to lose face and harden its audit position even more. Regarding language issues, Chinese is one of the United Nations' six official languages, but it is difficult to learn for non-Asian students. It is based on logograms and pictographs, not traditional letters as in Western languages, and within one Chinese language there are at least ten major dialect groups – in essence, ten further Chinese languages.

Of the four problem areas identified in the PricewaterhouseCoopers survey of 2006, both cultural and language issues can be minimized with an effort on the part of TNC managers. The problems that remain are the rapidly evolving Chinese tax and transfer pricing regulations and the lag in consistent interpretation of those regulations by tax authorities throughout China.

Any TNC executives new to doing business in Asia Pacific in general, and China in particular, should read *International Transfer Pricing in Asia Pacific* (2005) by Jian Li and Alan Paisey for an excellent grounding in the similarities and differences in tax and transfer pricing regimes across major Asia Pacific countries, including China. Once familiar with transfer pricing in Asia Pacific, the reader will find *Transfer Pricing Audits in China* to be a natural extension of this previous text by these authors, narrowing in as it does on issues that relate to TNCs with subsidiaries or affiliates in China. Building on what was discussed about China and transfer pricing in the first book, the topics covered in this book give the reader a thorough grounding in the specific transfer pricing issues that will arise for a TNC in the course of its business in China, both from the Chinese and the TNC's own viewpoints.

Understanding the nuts and bolts of China's audit approach will not guarantee that a TNC will not be audited by the SAT, or, if audited, that the outcome with be favourable. What Jian Li and Alan Paisey have done is to give TNC managers the tools to level the audit playing field. The first part of the text reviews foreign direct investments and enterprises, and relates them to transfer pricing. It is then that the reader is introduced to the mechanics of the audit, starting with both Chinese and non-Chinese transfer pricing regimes. The authors work their way through documentation requirements, which definitely vary by country. For example, if a TNC has subsidiaries in two countries, one which requires contemporaneous documentation and another that does not, it is essential that the former country's documentation requirements be met, or else the TNC is inviting an audit and penalties. Li and Paisey assume that once a TNC is comfortable with the transfer pricing requirements of its subsidiaries in China, an APA with the SAT is the next logical step. While an APA allows the TNC and the SAT to agree on an acceptable transfer pricing method for certain transactions for a multi-year period, it does not mean that the TNC will not be audited. What an APA does ensure is that, if the TNC is audited, the transfer pricing method used will be acceptable and not an audit issue.

When finished with this book, the reader will more fully understand the transfer pricing environment in China and transfer pricing issues from a distinctly Chinese vantage point. A TNC armed with this detailed knowledge about China's tax and transfer pricing regime will have a competitive advantage in a difficult but rewarding market environment.

Susan Borkowski
La Salle University
Philadelphia
July 2006

References

Ernst & Young (2005) *Global Transfer Pricing Trends, Practices and Analysis*. November, EYG No. CS0005.

Kral, Mark E. (2005) *Transfer Pricing as an International Tax Strategy Stop*. May. http://www.rsmmcgladrey.com/Generated_HTML/News/Webinar_5_09_05.html

PricewaterhouseCoopers (2006) *Managing and Planning for Tax in Asia Pacific* http://www.pwc.com/extweb/pwcpublications.nsf/docid/28ADED63DD2AE09 2CA257170001351CF

Ring, Diane (2002) *One Nation among Many: Policy Implications of Cross-Border Tax Arbitrage*. 44 Boston College Law Review 79 (December): 79–175.

Part I
Field of Audit

1
Foreign Direct Investments and Enterprises

Introduction

The world economy has become largely globalized, multinational enterprises contributing a substantial portion to the world's total trade. They have of themselves become significant and powerful elements in the world's economic and political landscape, helping to carry the intricacies and dynamics of international business and international relations to unprecedented levels of complexity and interrelatedness. One of the greatest exemplars of this development is the Siemens Corporation which in 2005 has reported itself as consisting of over 900 fully owned and over 400 majority-owned subsidiaries or joint ventures.

The hallmark of the operations of the multinational enterprise, and the means by which they must typically act, is their practice of making direct investments of assets of one kind or another in the economies of nations other than those of their own origins. Whilst the pace and extent of such globalization may be approaching its zenith in the face of resurgent nationalism – at least in some parts of the world – the process in the case of China is still in the direction of increasing foreign investment.

Multinational enterprises have distinctive features that set them apart from their exclusively national, domestic counterparts. Multinational enterprises consider the global economy as a single market place. They integrate their production and trading on a worldwide scale, rather than within the confines of individual countries. They internalize trading and investment within a multinational system. Compared with domestic companies, multinational enterprises consequently face more complex management problems in having to deal with a variety of political regimes, legal systems, labour markets, and currencies.

Among the many variables that they constantly face is the crucial issue of taxation, which has a pervasive influence on all their multifarious operations. Tax levels, in forming at least a potential operational deterrent, are therefore an important consideration, giving rise to the search for means to avoid or evade tax liabilities.

One means for achieving this objective lies to hand in the need for, or possibility of, the transfer of assets between constituent units of the same company located in different countries. Transactions between such constituent parts of a company in different countries have to be subject to internal company pricing carrying the convenient nomenclatural term of transfer pricing. This pricing for both sales and purchases relates to the profitability of any company unit involved and therefore to its tax liabilities. It follows that transfer pricing, as the decisional process and final prices charged to assets passing between companies or operational units that are related to each other – but are located in different countries – is one of the most important concerns for multinational enterprises in their dealings with their fiscal liabilities.

Theories of foreign direct investment

Theories explaining and describing the nature and function of the multinational enterprise and foreign direct investment have been advanced over several recent decades. The literature includes contributions by a number of economists, including Coase (1937), Vernon (1971), Buckley and Casson (1976), Hymer (1976), Dunning (1980), Kindleberger (1984), Dunning and Rugman (1985), Corley (1992), and Caves (1996).

Hymer (1976) established a theory of imperfect competition and monopoly advantages to explain the reason for the existence of multinational enterprises. In his dissertation 'The international operations of national firms: a study of direct foreign investment', he argued that a perfectly competitive market is only possible in theory. In the real world, the market is imperfect. Because of their unfamiliarity with local market conditions, multinational enterprises engaging in international production are at a disadvantage when compared with local firms. To compete successfully with local firms in a host country environment, multinational enterprises must be able to exploit certain specific advantages not possessed by their local competitors. Market imperfections, created by the existence of some monopolistic or oligopolistic advantages of multinational enterprises, provide them with compensating advantages that exceed the disadvantages of being in a host country.

Since market imperfections offer multinational enterprises competitive advantages over indigenous firms, these advantages must be held monopolistically. In other words, these advantages must not be obtainable by their local competitors. Otherwise, their specific advantages could be neutralized over time. To survive in foreign markets, multinational enterprises must therefore install effective barriers to the entry of local competitors by internalizing markets across national boundaries.

Hymer's theory is based upon the concept of structural market failure and, therefore, is restricted to the structural aspect of market imperfections. The elements of structural market imperfections include economies of scale, knowledge advantages, distribution networks, product diversification, and credit advantages.

Dunning and Rugman (1985) noted that Hymer (1976) had not taken account of the distinction between structural (endogenous) and transaction-cost (cognitive or exogenous) market imperfections and, hence, had overlooked the work of Coase (1937), who had emphasized the transaction-cost side of market imperfections and the importance of internal markets. Coase's (1937) theory originally applied to multi-plant indigenous firms. He suggested that because the external market mechanism inflicts higher transaction costs on processes and obligations – such as defining and accepting contractual obligations, fixing contract prices, and taxes to be paid on market transactions – a firm may organize these activities internally in response to the transaction costs, creating an integrated internal market.

Buckley and Casson (1976) developed this theory into an explanation for multinational enterprise activities. They stressed the importance of market imperfections in intermediate product markets, particularly those of patented technical knowledge, and human capital, concluding that such imperfections provided an incentive for a multinational enterprise to internalize resource markets.

Perhaps the most influential work on the subject of a multinational's international production, however, was Dunning's (1980) eclectic paradigm. This paradigm is an attempt to synthesize the essential features of the multinational enterprise and foreign direct investment theories. Dunning's 'eclectic theory of international production' has three dimensions, namely:

1. Ownership specific advantages (competitive advantages). These advantages explain the reasons for international production. A multinational enterprise possesses ownership advantages that may be held temporarily or permanently, but are held exclusively. They

are also called 'monopoly advantages'. For example, securing a monopoly of intangible assets or economies of scale provides an organization with a competitive edge over indigenous firms in the foreign market.
2. Location specific advantages (configuration advantages). These advantages explain the choice of locations of international production. They consist of factors specific to a particular place. The home or host country itself, therefore, rather than the multinational enterprise, contributes to these advantages. Location advantages include, but are not limited to, the host nation's economic system, government policies, sources of materials, market structure, labour supply, and the availability of infrastructural assets – such as commercial, legal, educational, transport, and communication services.
3. Internalization specific advantages (coordinating advantages). These advantages explain the method of international production. Multinational enterprises operating in host countries inevitably face market imperfections caused by government regulations or natural externalities in the transfer of all kinds of assets. The main advantage of a multinational enterprise is its ability to use the internal markets within the same firm to overcome market imperfections in the host environment.

Dunning's eclectic paradigm emphasizes exogenous market imperfections, which are classic reasons for the internalization of markets by multinational enterprises and the motive for foreign direct investment. A multinational enterprise which seeks to enter a foreign market has a choice of three approaches – namely exporting, foreign direct investment, or licensing. As international business increases, of these three options, foreign direct investment has become the preferred choice by multinational enterprises in general.

Market imperfections are advanced to explain the need of foreign direct investment as a means to enter the economy of a foreign country rather than exporting or licensing. In a perfectly competitive market, a firm can buy or sell goods and services at market prices. Foreign markets can be serviced by exports or licensing. Nevertheless, perfect competition is not common in practice. Rather, markets are imperfect and often inflict high transaction costs on transfers of goods and services. In response to market imperfections in foreign countries, therefore, a multinational enterprise internalizes its trade transactions by using a hierarchical structure to control its international production, thereby minimizing transaction costs. Internalization takes the form of foreign direct investment when there are barriers to trade which preclude exporting, or risk reducing, and when there are firm-specific advantages for the multinational enterprise, such as technological knowledge, management skills, or market know-how, which discourage licensing.

It can be concluded that foreign direct investment occurs as a response to both natural and unnatural market imperfections. In short, foreign direct investment is determined by the need to internalize a firm-specific advantage to overcome market imperfections. The result of it has been a greatly increased volume of international trade.

Dunning's (1980) theory explains why multinational enterprises establish cross-border subsidiaries through foreign direct investment. According to Dunning's theory of market imperfections and internalization, multinational enterprises take a number of considerations into account when determining the extent of their foreign direct investment and international operations. These considerations generally include ownership advantages, location advantages, and internalization advantages. Multinational enterprises can exploit market imperfections to achieve ownership, location, and internalization advantages. Furthermore, multinational enterprises can manage transfer prices according to their perspectives on how best to meet various market imperfections.

Trends and patterns in china

The two primary government agencies in China involved in permitting, regulating, and managing foreign investment enterprises at national level are the Ministry of Commerce and the State Administration for Industry and Commerce. Each of these national authorities has a network of Provincial Departments covering the whole country. They are charged with the task of implementing and enforcing the lawful policies adopted at national level, but in addition they are empowered to formulate supplementary policies for their own provinces as required for the discharge of this responsibility.

Foreign direct investment in China has undergone a rapid growth since 1992. From the beginning in 1993, China has emerged as the largest single recipient of foreign direct investment among the developing countries, by 2001 becoming the second largest recipient of foreign direct investment in the world, behind the United States.

With its accession to the World Trade Organization in December 2001, the amount of foreign direct investment in China jumped to US$ 52.74 billion in the following year, a year of great significance in

Table 1.1 Foreign direct investment in China, 1990–2004

Year	Number of projects	Contractual value (US$ billion)	Realized value (US$ billion)
1990	7,273	6.596	3.487
1991	12,978	11.977	4.366
1992	48,764	58.124	11.008
1993	83,437	111.436	27.515
1994	47,549	82.680	33.767
1995	37,011	91.282	37.521
1996	24,556	73.236	41.726
1997	21,001	51.003	45.257
1998	19,799	52.102	45.463
1999	16,918	41.223	40.319
2000	22,347	62.380	40.715
2001	26,140	69.195	46.878
2002	34,171	82.768	52.743
2003	41,081	115.07	53.505
2004	43,664	153.479	60.630

Source: Ministry of Commerce of the People's Republic of China's website. The website address is http://www.mofcom.gov.cn

that this additional investment enabled China to surpass the United States to become the world's largest recipient of foreign direct investment. The accumulated total from 1979 to 2004 was US$ 562.101 billion.

As shown in Table 1.1, over the last decade or so (1990–2004), the number and volume of foreign direct investments have dramatically increased in China. The number of foreign direct investment projects increased from 7,273 in 1990 to 43,664 in 2004. The contractual value of foreign direct investment projects increased from US$ 6.596 billion in 1990 to US$ 153.479 billion in 2004. The realized value of all foreign direct investment projects increased from US$ 3.487 billion in 1990 to US$ 60.630 billion in 2004. Future foreign direct investment is likely to reach US$ 100 billion per year.

Legal forms of foreign direct investment. The Chinese government allows three types of foreign investment enterprises to operate in China, as follows.

- Wholly foreign-owned enterprises (WFOE)
- Joint ventures – which may be either equity joint ventures (EJV), contractual joint ventures (CJV), or joint explorations (JE)
- Share companies with foreign investments (SCWFI).

Table 1.2 Forms of foreign direct investment to December 2004 (US$ billion)

Legal Form	Number of projects	Percentage	Contractual value	Percentage	Realized value	Percentage
WFOE	202,816	39.85	531.43	48.46	239.22	42.59
EJV	249,974	49.19	380.7	34.72	223.98	39.89
CJV	55,855	10.98	178.59	16.29	89.73	15.98
JE	191	0.04	4.74	0.43	7.51	1.34
SCWFI	80	0.02	1.16	0.11	1.11	0.19
Total	508,916	100	1096.52	100	561.55	100

Source: Ministry of Commerce of the People's Republic of China's website.
The website address is http://www.mofcom.gov.cn

As shown in the shaded part of Table 1.2, wholly foreign-owned enterprises have been the most popular form of foreign direct investment so far, making up about 42.59% of the realized value of foreign direct investments. Other important forms of foreign direct investment are equity joint venture and contractual joint venture. Respectively they account for 39.89% and 15.98% of the cumulative actual foreign direct investment.

Now that the Chinese government has abolished the restrictions on the freedom of wholly foreign-owned enterprises to sell their products in the domestic market, however, multinationals are more likely to favour their presence in China as wholly foreign-owned enterprises to avoid the conflicts of interest that might arise with Chinese partners if they established themselves on any other basis.

The sources of foreign direct investment. Table 1.3 shows the extent of foreign direct investment in China made by the top ten countries or other quasi-foreign territorial sources, as they stood at the end of 2004. The largest source of foreign direct investment is Hong Kong, accounting for 48.96% of accumulated actual foreign direct investment during the period 1979–2004. Hong Kong is followed by the United States (9.73%), Japan (9.49%), Taiwan (8.03%), the Virgin Islands (7.48%), Korea (5.26%), Singapore (5.18%), the United Kingdom (2.48%), Germany (2.01%), and France (1.38%).

The share of foreign direct investment from Hong Kong is so high for several reasons. First, a number of western multinational companies have formed joint ventures with Hong Kong firms to invest in China and utilize the experience and expertise of Hong Kong managers in the Chinese market. Second, many Taiwanese companies, instead of investing directly, invest in China via Hong Kong for political reasons. Third, it is estimated that since 1992 much of the investment from

Table 1.3 Foreign direct investment from the top ten countries to December 2004 (US$ billion)

Source	Realized value	Percentage
Hong Kong	241.574	48.96
United States	48.029	9.73
Japan	46.846	9.49
Taiwan	39.605	8.03
Virgin Islands	36.895	7.48
Korea	25.935	5.26
Singapore	25.539	5.18
United Kingdom	12.231	2.48
Germany	9.909	2.01
France	6.804	1.38
Total	493.367	100

Source: Invest in China website. The address is http://www.fdi.gov.cn

Table 1.4 Regional distribution of actual foreign direct investment to December 2004

Region	Number of projects	Percentage	Contractual value	Percentage	Realized value	Percentage
Eastern	419,505	82.43	951.589	86.78	484.813	86.25
Central	56,195	11.04	84.339	7.69	51.470	9.16
Western	33,241	6.53	60.681	5.53	25.817	4.59
Total	508,941	100	1096.608	100	562.101	100

Source: Invest in China website. The website address is http://www.fdi.gov.cn
Note:
The Eastern Region includes: Beijing, Tianjin, Hebei, Liaoning, Shanghai, Jiangsu, Guangdong, Zhejiang, Fujian, Shandong, and Hainan.
The Central Region includes: Shanxi, Jilin, Heilongjiang, Anhui, Jiangxi, Shanxi, Henan, Hubei, and Hunan.
The Western Region includes: Inner Mongolia, Guangxi, Sichuan, Chongqing, Guizhou, Yunnan, Shanxi, Gansu, Qinghai, Ningxia, Xinjiang, and Tibet.

Hong Kong has been actually a recycling of capital from mainland China, which sought to take advantage of the preferential policies offered to foreign investors. The overall product range represented by the investments of Taiwanese firms is similar to those of Hong Kong. However, from the mid-1990s onwards, investments from Taiwan rapidly expanded into technology-intensive sectors such as information technology.

The Chinese government has been abolishing restrictions on foreign companies conducting business in China. Large western multinationals can now be directly involved in business activities in China. As a result, in the past decade, Hong Kong's share of the total foreign direct investment has significantly decreased, while the shares of the United States and the European Union have greatly increased. Since China's accession to the World Trade Organization in December 2001, this trend has continued.

Distribution of actual foreign direct investment in China. It may be seen in Table 1.4, that in 32 provinces, including five Autonomous Regions – Xinjiang, Tibet, Ningxia, Guangxi, and the Inner Mongolia Autonomous Region – and four Municipalities – Beijing, Tianjin, Shanghai, and Chongqing – the distribution of foreign direct investment is quantified according to three regions of China – the Eastern Region, the Central Region, and the Western Region. The Eastern Region dominates the market for inward foreign direct investment over other provincial groupings. Within the Eastern Region, Guangdong, Jiangsu, Fujian, and Shanghai are the four biggest recipients of foreign direct investment among the numerous cities of the Region's provinces that have a share of it. By 2004, the eastern region had taken 86.25% of the total cumulative actual investment.

The share of cumulative actual foreign direct investment in the Central Region gradually increased from 5% during the 1980s to 9.16% by the end of 2004. The main recipient provinces in it are Henan, Hubei, and Hunan. The less developed Western Region receives only 4.59% of the cumulative actual direct investment, Sichuan and Shanxi attracting more foreign direct investment inflows than other provinces in this Region. Although the export-oriented foreign investments are concentrated in the Eastern Region of China, the distribution of foreign direct investment inflows has spread from its initial establishment in the coastal provinces to the Region's inland provinces. Emerging domestic markets, industrial advantages, and available labour, as well as the developing infrastructure of inland provinces, however, are beginning to offer opportunities that will help to attract proportionately more locally market-oriented foreign direct investments to these inland provinces in the future.

At present, the top 500 multinational enterprises in the world have established subsidiaries or branches in China. Table 1.5 depicts the provincial distribution of actual foreign direct investment by these top 500 multinationals in China in 2002. The overall pattern of distribution is similar to that for all companies as shown in Table 1.4. The multinational companies are concentrated in the eastern provinces, of which Shanghai, Guangdong, Beijing and Jiangsu have attracted more

Table 1.5 The provincial distribution of actual foreign direct investment by the top 500 multinationals in 2002

Province	Number of projects	Percentage	Province	Number of projects	Percentage
Shanghai	689	23.7	Fujian	68	2.3
Guangdong	524	18.0	Hebei	53	1.8
Beijing	412	14.2	Hubei	51	1.7
Jiangsu	390	13.4	Chongqing	41	1.4
Tianjin	179	6.2	Sichuan	39	1.3
Liaoning	169	5.8	Hainan	18	0.6
Shandong	156	5.4	Guangxi	14	0.5
Zhejiang	102	3.5	Total	2905	100

Source: *The world's top 500 multinational companies operating in China.* (2ed.) (2003). ShangDong, China: People's Publisher of ShangDong (in Chinese), p. 5.

foreign direct investment than other provinces or cities. The proportional shares of the projects of foreign direct investment in these four provinces/cities being respectively 23.7%, 18%, 14.2% and 13.4%.

The distribution of actual foreign direct investment according to industry. Table 1.6 provides basic statistics on the distribution of actual foreign direct investment according to industry. Foreign direct investment stocks concentrate on manufacturing industry. The traditional labour-intensive manufacturing industries, such as Clothing Products, Furniture, Cultural Goods, Educational Goods, Sports Goods, Leather, Furs, and Down and Related Products, continue to be the main industries of foreign direct investment inflows. Foreign direct investment inflows also continue to favour those industries with high output and low tax liabilities, such as Electronic and Telecommunications Equipment, Precision Instruments, Meters, and Office Electrical Equipment. In recent years, however, as the Chinese government adopts polices which encourage foreign direct investments in high technology industries, investments from large multinational firms are expanding into technology-intensive industries.

A number of multinationals have chosen China as a site for their regional headquarters or as Research and Development (R&D) centres. Since Motorola established the first research and development department in 1993 in China, over 700 foreign research and development laboratories have been set up in the country. The latest example is Ericsson – the world's largest maker of mobile phone networks – which announced in September 2005 it would invest US$ 1 billion in manu-

Table 1.6 Distribution of actual foreign direct investment to December 2003 according to industry (US$ 100 million)

Industry	Contractual value	Percentage
Agriculture, Forestry, Poultry and Livestock Farming, and Fishing	180.6	1.91
Mining	16.1	0.8
Manufacturing	6003.8	63.66
Electricity, Gas and Water Supply	56.2	0.6
Construction	242.9	2.57
Transport, Storage, and Postage	238.2	2.52
Wholesale and Retail Trades	288.2	3.6
Banking	8.5	0.9
Real Estate	1808.6	19.8
Property and Business Services	301.7	3.2
Scientific Research, Technical and Mineral Exploration Services	41.9	0.44
Personal and Other Services	163.9	1.73
Education	5.6	0.27
Health, Social Security, and Welfare	54.3	0.58
Total	9,410.5	100

Source: *The world's top 500 multinational companies operating in China.* (2ed.) (2003). ShangDong, China: People's Publisher of ShangDong (in Chinese), p. 5.

facturing and research in China over the next five years. In addition, as the Chinese government lifts the access restrictions on foreign companies whose businesses lie in some of the traditionally state controlled service sectors such as Financing and Insurance, Telecommunications, Commerce, and Transport, even more opportunities will be available to foreign companies. The services industry is expected to become the new focus of investment from large multinational companies in China in the near future (Lai, 2002).

Table 1.7 provides further details of the distribution of actual foreign direct investment according to industry by showing the contribution made by the top 500 multinationals in China in 2002. These large companies concentrate on industries with economies of scale, such as automotive manufacturing. Among the top 500 multinationals, 24 are exclusively involved in motor products and 27 in motor products and related products. The large motor companies have already established 207 subsidiaries in China. In the services sector, 80% of the increasing investment in services, such as financing and insurance, is concentrated and spreading in Beijing, Shanghai, Guangdong and Tianjin.

Table 1.7 Distribution of actual foreign direct investment by the top 500 multinationals in China in 2002 according to industry

Industry	Number of projects	Percentage	Industry	Number of projects	Percentage
Investment	91	3.4	Telecommunication Equipment	105	3.9
R&D Centres	54	2.0	Computers and Software	100	3.7
Petroleum Extraction	131	4.8	Construction Materials	57	2.1
Electronic and Electrical Equipment	407	15.0	Medical	66	2.4
Transport Equipment	218	8.1	Finance, Insurance and Leasing	160	5.9
Petrochemicals and Chemicals	213	7.9	International Trade	121	4.5
Metal Processing and Hardware	192	7.1	Logistics	88	3.3
Textiles and Garments	154	5.7	Wholesale and Retail Trades	74	2.7
Food and Beverage	142	5.2	Infrastructure	60	2.2
Light Industry	124	4.6	Real Estate	41	1.5
Instruments and Meters	109	4.0	Total	2707	100

Source: *The world's top 500 multinational companies operating in China*. (2ed.) (2003). ShangDong, China: People's Publisher of ShangDong (in Chinese), p. 5.

Foreign direct investment and foreign trade

The rapid expansion of foreign investment enterprises has contributed significantly to the increase in international trade by China. Nowadays, foreign investment enterprises have become the main element driving its foreign trade growth. Table 1.8 depicts the overall trends in total exports and imports compared with the imports and exports by foreign investment enterprises only during the period 1990 to 2004. Over this period, China's exports increased from US$ 62.09 billion to US$ 593.37 billion, while imports increased from US$ 53.35 billion to US$ 561.42 billion.

Table 1.8 Portions of China's total exports and imports contributed by foreign investment enterprises (FIEs) 1990–2004 (US$ billion)

Year	Exports (national totals)	Exports by FIEs	Percentage	Imports (national totals)	Imports by FIEs	Percentage	Balance of trade
1990	62.09	7.81	12.58	53.35	12.30	23.06	8.74
1991	71.91	12.05	16.75	63.79	16.91	26.51	8.12
1992	84.94	17.36	20.44	80.59	26.39	32.74	4.35
1993	91.74	25.24	27.51	103.96	41.83	40.24	-12.22
1994	121.01	34.71	28.69	115.62	52.94	45.78	5.39
1995	148.77	46.88	31.51	132.08	62.94	47.66	16.69
1996	151.07	61.51	40.71	138.84	75.60	54.45	12.23
1997	182.70	74.90	41.00	142.36	77.72	54.59	40.34
1998	183.75	80.96	44.06	140.17	76.72	54.73	43.58
1999	194.93	88.63	45.47	165.72	85.88	51.83	29.21
2000	249.20	119.44	47.93	225.09	117.27	52.10	24.11
2001	266.16	133.24	50.10	243.61	125.86	51.70	22.55
2002	325.57	169.94	52.20	295.22	160.29	54.29	30.35
2003	438.37	240.34	54.83	412.84	231.91	56.18	25.53
2004	593.37	338.61	57.07	561.42	324.56	57.81	31.95

Source: Invest in China website. The website address is http://www.fdi.gov.cn.

Among the factors promoting both export and import growth, foreign direct investment has played an important part. During the period 1990 to 2004, the value of exports by foreign investment enterprises increased from US$ 7.81 billion to US$ 338.61 billion, and the value of imports by foreign investment enterprises increased from US$ 12.3 billion to US$ 324.56 billion. Foreign investment enterprises have become the major force behind the expansion of China's exporting and importing activities.

Consequently, the share of foreign investment enterprises in the total exports of China increased from 12.58% in 1990 to 57.07% in 2004 and of imports from 23.06% in 1990 to 57.81% in 2004. The impact of foreign direct investment on the trade balance of China has been of major importance. It is shown in Table 1.8, that except for the year 1993, as shaded – when the major cause of a trade deficit was a more than 50% surge in imports by foreign investment enterprises (Chan and Chow, 1998, p. 20) – China enjoyed a long period of trade surplus. Over the period 1990 to 1997, the imports of foreign investment enterprises constantly exceeded their exports. Since 1998, however, the situation has been reversed, the exports of foreign investment enterprises having exceeded their imports. Foreign direct investment has greatly increased the volume of Chinese overseas trade.

Table 1.9 Exports by foreign investment enterprises to the main countries or other destinations, 1991–1994 (US$ 100 million)

Destination	Hong Kong	Taiwan	Japan	European Union	USA	Totals
1991	53.23	N/A	12.18	4.57	9.28	N/A
1992	77.53	N/A	19.49	7.13	16.48	N/A
1993	66.14	5.62	54	28.94	67.35	222.05
1994	91.15	8.58	78.59	37.14	88.29	303.75
1995	119.6	11.5	109.8	48.21	111.89	401
1996	148.91	12.57	148.82	70.3	134.99	515.59
1997	183.37	15.97	160.09	91.36	168.74	619.53
1998	174.76	20.39	159.16	115.23	203.32	672.86
1999	180.44	19.86	176.82	126.60	225.50	729.22
2000	247.76	25.01	233.40	173.00	287.98	967.15
2001	285.07	25.61	264.04	192.77	298.76	1066.25
2002	369.71	37.6	299.86	239.46	405	1351.63
2003	506.24	56.92	380.23	395.14	576.69	1915.22
2004	691.57	84.31	480.38	571.58	822.71	2650.55

Source: Invest in China website. The website address is http://www.fdi.gov.cn.

Table 1.10 Imports by foreign investment enterprises from the main countries or other sources, 1991–1994 (US$ 100 million)

Sources	Hong Kong	Taiwan	Japan	European Union	USA	Totals
1991	45.91	N/A	25.78	23.47	10.84	N/A
1992	59.43	N/A	41.58	32.29	17.39	N/A
1993	51.26	90.67	105.18	63.99	34.20	345.30
1994	51.56	100.94	141.84	78.75	41.78	414.87
1995	49.70	104.48	170.30	149.13	53.47	527.08
1996	49.78	115.35	194.97	113.81	70.92	544.83
1997	44.04	113.23	195.09	106.15	75.82	534.33
1998	41.37	114.49	187.74	112.20	77.14	532.94
1999	41.48	127.60	214.34	124.96	83.10	591.50
2000	56.85	165.18	284.15	166.23	99.60	772.01
2001	56.86	178.89	288.97	185.77	115.69	826.18
2002	68.04	256.27	359.45	189.43	131.07	1004.26
2003	69.22	357.87	512.57	260.41	168.08	1368.15
2004	73.80	493.87	675.16	361.69	233.27	1837.79

Source: Invest in China website. The website address is http://www.fdi.gov.cn.

Exports and imports by foreign investment enterprises. Tables 1.9 and 1.10 respectively show exports to the main countries or other destinations, and imports from the main countries or other sources, by foreign investment enterprises which are also China's major trading partners. Given that the share of the exports and imports by foreign investment enterprises in the nation's total exports and imports account for a significant proportion of it, it is not surprising to find that the overall pattern of exports and imports by foreign investment enterprises is similar to that of the national exports and imports totals overall. The United States is the most important export market of the foreign investment enterprises, followed by Hong Kong, the European Union, and Japan. Japan is the largest source of imports by foreign investment enterprises to China, followed by Taiwan, and the European Union. The investments from Hong Kong are dominated by export-oriented, labour-intensive manufacturing industry.

Summary

Hand in hand with the increasing globalization of commercial activity during recent decades has been the spectacular rise of China to a position of economic power. The reasons for it include the resolve of successive governments of China to ensure that their country takes a full and normal part in international commerce, the size of the country's population making it the largest single national market in the world, and the responsive eagerness of enterprises from all other parts of the world to obtain a share in that market.

The great variety and number of the foreign enterprises which have taken advantage of the inducements and encouragement offered by the Chinese government are outlined, together with an indication of the impact they have made on the Chinese economy.

2
Transfer Pricing in Concept

Introduction

Transfer pricing is the term given to the process and determination of pricing the assets transferred between related firms of a multinational company across different tax jurisdictions. Multinational subsidiaries can be located in a variety of different foreign countries. They may sell their own finished products direct to their own foreign markets or to affiliates for marketing, and or semi-finished products to related companies in their own multinational group as part of a collective production and distribution system involving company units in more than one country. Assets other than physical products that enter into or relate to production and sales are also subject to such transfers.

Global group profit maximization and correlated tax minimization are the major objectives of multinational enterprises. The differentiation of corporate tax systems and corporate income tax rates to be found between countries across the world provide enormous tax liability planning opportunities for multinationals to manipulate their global tax liabilities through adroit transfer pricing decisions – to their own advantage, but to the disadvantage of national governments of the countries in which their subsidiaries are operating.

Company international tax planning

Generally, the two types of tax imposed on companies are direct taxes and indirect taxes. Direct taxes are those imposed on the company's income – such as corporate income tax, capital gains tax, and withholding tax. Indirect taxes are those imposed on certain transactions of a company – such as value added tax, consumption tax, and business tax. With respect to indirect taxes, the system of taxation is generally particular to the individual country concerned. Tax planning opportunities in relation to such taxes usually arise purely on a domestic basis. International tax planning, therefore, concentrates primarily on planning techniques relating to direct taxes.

Multinational enterprises are organizations that engage in production or service activities in two or more countries. A substantial part of international trade consists of high volumes of intercompany sales, or commercial transactions between parent companies and their foreign affiliates and branches, or between their several subsidiaries. Multinational tax planning generally revolves around mechanisms that may be adopted to minimize the overall worldwide tax liabilities imposed on a multinational company at each of the following three levels.

1. **Taxation in the host country as the source of profits.** At the level where operating profits are earned by subsidiaries and branches in various host countries, the taxes involved will typically be corporate income taxes, capital gains taxes, and local income taxes.
2. **Intermediate taxation on remitted profits.** Taxes are imposed on the profits repatriated by subsidiaries operating in host countries to their parent companies in their home countries. Such intermediate taxes are typically withholding taxes in the host country as the source of the profits.
3. **Taxation on profits repatriated to the home country.** Taxes are imposed on profits in the home country of a parent company that have been repatriated from its operating subsidiaries or other entities in other countries. Additionally, in some cases home country taxes may be imposed on foreign profits which have not been repatriated – in circumstances where anti-tax haven legislation may apply (Tomsett, 1989, pp. 3–4).

In most countries across the world, the important *a priori* assumptions are made in the case of international taxation that each country is entitled to extend its tax jurisdiction to the income of non-residents that is sourced in other countries, and to the non-exempt worldwide income of resident companies, although a home country resident's tax liability is generally reduced by the amount of any foreign tax already paid. In practice, the loopholes, opportunities, anomalies, and provisos that inevitably arise from the vast range of national variations in taxation regulations, present any company operating in several countries with the need to give explicit attention to the formulation of strategies for dealing with its multifarious tax liabilities.

A multinational parent company can design its international tax planning strategies in terms of three factors – its choice of organizational form, a time period, and its capital structure. Each of these can have its own effects on taxation liabilities as follows.

- **The choice of organizational form.** The multinational in designing its organizational form for embarking on a foreign operation through an overseas branch, a subsidiary, or a partnership, needs to consider the tax implications of the choice made. If the multinational organizes its foreign affiliate as a branch, the parent company can claim a tax credit for foreign taxes paid by the branch or can deduct the foreign losses of the branch against the parent's home country taxable income. However, this organizational form would result in the inclusion of all branch income in the worldwide income of the parent company, even if the branch did not remit any profits. In contrast, if the multinational organizes its foreign affiliate as a subsidiary, the parent may be allowed to defer a recognition of income from the subsidiary. The disadvantage is that dividends paid by the subsidiary are subjected to foreign withholding taxes. Additionally, operating losses generated by the foreign subsidiary cannot be passed to the parent company. The multinational may instead elect to form partnerships where any income or loss will flow directly through the partners without creating tax impositions on the foreign entity itself.
- **Time period.** A foreign subsidiary is a separate legal entity from its parent. Most home countries do not tax foreign business profits earned through a foreign subsidiary until the subsidiary distributes those earnings to the parent as a dividend. The parent may defer as long as possible the recognition of income from the subsidiary and the payment of tax until dividends are distributed to the parent. This is a particularly advantageous practice if the host country has a low tax rate.
- **Capital structure.** One of the fundamental choices for a parent firm is how to finance its foreign entities. The capital structure of its foreign entities can affect the tax situation of the multinational as a whole. Financing through debt or equity will have different tax effects related to the deductibility of interest expenses and the lack of deductibility for equity contributions. The parent can use debt to finance its foreign affiliates in high tax countries, and equity to finance its subsidiaries in low tax countries.

Multinational tax management perspective

Perhaps the most critical mechanism to hand for multinational tax planning is transfer pricing. Transfer pricing in principle generates significant tax planning implications for multinational enterprises. From the perspective of tax management alone, transfer pricing practices can be designed to meet the objectives of worldwide income tax minimization, import duties minimization, withholding tax minimization, and foreign tax credit maximization.

Minimization of worldwide income tax. Since corporate income tax rates vary between countries, a multinational enterprise can use its internal pricing system to shift taxable income from a country with a high tax rate to a country with a lower tax rate. The overall effect is that the multinational enterprise as a whole can minimize its global tax payments. There are four ways in which a multinational enterprise can use transfer prices to manipulate its income tax payments in this way, as follows.

1. A multinational enterprise operating in a high tax rate country imports tangible assets such as raw materials and equipment from its associated enterprise operating in a low tax country at a high price, or exports such goods to the affiliated firm abroad at a low price.
2. A multinational enterprise operating in a high tax rate country pays excessively high royalties or other fees to its associated enterprise for the use of intangible property, such as patents and know-how, owned by the foreign associated enterprise, or sells such intangible property to the associated enterprise at unreasonably low prices.
3. A multinational enterprise operating in a high tax rate country provides services, such as management expertise and marketing advice, to its associated enterprise operating in a low tax country free of charge or with unreasonably low fees, or pays excessively high fees for such services provided by the associated enterprise.
4. A multinational enterprise operating in a high tax rate country borrows funds from its associated enterprise operating in a low tax country and pays an excessive interest rate on the loan, or makes loans available to its associated enterprise at unreasonably low rates of interest.

Transfer prices can be variously manipulated by effecting transactions in all four of the above categories to shift profits from a company

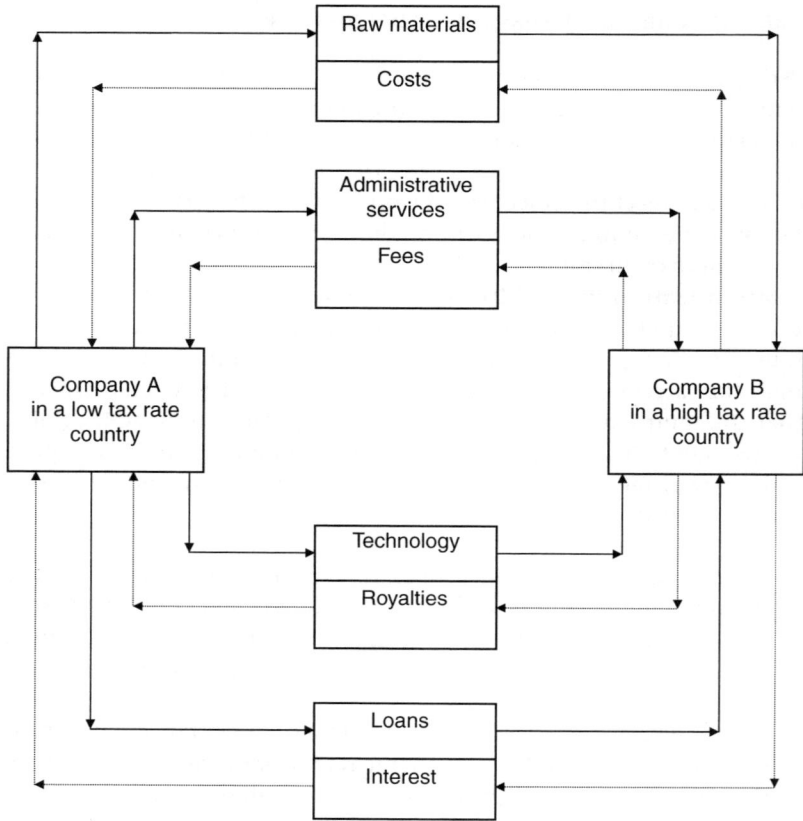

Figure 2.1 Transfer pricing model for two company units located in different countries

Note: Solid arrows represent the transfer of assets, dotted arrows the transfer of payments

located in a high tax rate country to an associated company in a low tax rate country as illustrated in the model in Figure 2.1.

Table 2.1 provides a further analysis of the effects of transfer pricing manoeuvres for tax savings within the multinational company as a whole. In the case illustrated, a parent company in the home country has two subsidiaries A and B, located, respectively, in the host countries α and β. Subsidiary A produces an intermediate product to be sold to subsidiary B, the latter processing the intermediate goods into a final product for sale in its local market. The products transferred have an open market price. The corporate tax rate in host country α is 20%, but 33% in the host country β.

Transfer Pricing in Concept 23

Table 2.1 Market price versus manipulated transfer price

Situation 1 Open market price
Subsidiary A sells to subsidiary B at the open market price $120,000.

Subsidiary A			Subsidiary B
A's manufacturing costs	$100,000		
A's open market price	$120,000 →	$120,000	B's purchase price paid to A
		$200,000	B's sale price to public
A's profit	$20,000	$80,000	B's profit
A's Tax payment (20%)	$4,000	$26,400	B's tax payment (33%)

Total tax payments: $4,000 + $26,400 = $30,400.

Situation 2: Transfer pricing manoeuvre
Subsidiary A sells to subsidiary B at the manipulated new sale (transfer) price $150,000.

Subsidiary A			Subsidiary B
A's manufacturing costs	$100,000		
A's new sale price	$150,000 →	$150,000	B's purchase price paid to A
		$200,000	B's sale price to public
A's profit	$50,000	$50,000	B's profit
A's Tax payment (20%)	$10,000	$16,500	B's tax payment (33%)

Total tax payments: $10,000 + $16,500 = $26,500.

In the first instance, the subsidiary A sells to subsidiary B at the open market price of $120,000. Subsidiary B sells the final product to public consumers at $200,000. The taxable incomes for subsidiaries A and B are $20,000 and $80,000, respectively. With the tax rate of 20% for subsidiary A and 33% for subsidiary B, subsidiary A pays $4,000 in income tax and subsidiary B pays $26,400. Altogether the total income tax payment of the multinational enterprise as a whole is therefore $4,000 + $26,400 = $30,400.

In the second instance, to reduce worldwide tax liabilities, with all other factors being equal, the parent company would allow its subsidiary A in the low tax country α to sell its products to its related subsidiary B in the high tax country β at the high price of $150,000. This higher product price in effect transfers income from subsidiary B to subsidiary A. The multinational as a whole can thereby minimize its total tax payments by shifting its profits to the lower tax jurisdiction country α. By such a transfer pricing manoeuvre, the multinational can save on its corporate tax liability, a saving calculated as $30,400 − $26,500 = $3,900.

Tax havens. A multinational enterprise can establish a subsidiary firm in a tax haven for tax planning purposes, tax havens being foreign countries or regions with low or zero corporate tax rates, legislation that supports banking and business secrecy, advanced communication facilities, and self-promotion as an offshore financial centre (Hines and Rice, 1994). Some 70 tax havens around the world exist to offer secrecy, low local taxes and costs, and the means for a foreign enterprise to avoid tax liabilities in its home country. The vehicle for this in the tax haven may consist of little more than a shell company, lacking local assets, employees, and all the normal physical manifestations of an established company. Its bank accounts are then used for the transfers of sums between associated companies for their mutual interests and purposes. Both legal monies and illegal monies can be involved, the latter for the purpose of obfuscation. Tax haven shell companies can be fronted by local banks, lawyers, and accountants to conceal their true ownership.

By transferring profits from high tax rate countries to a tax haven, the multinational can enjoy considerable tax savings. As an example, in Figure 2.2, the parent company in a high tax rate country sells goods to its foreign affiliate X in a country with a high tax rate. Instead of directly charging affiliate X with an open market price for the goods, the parent company invoices its second subsidiary Y established in a tax haven at a low price. Subsequently, subsidiary Y invoices subsidiary X for the same goods sent from the parent company to company X at a high price. In this way, profits are transferred from the parent company and company X to company Y. Since company Y is located in the tax haven with a very low or zero tax rate, the multinational enterprise as a whole can minimize its income tax payments.

In terms of its functions, company Y is the central financial subsidiary of the group and may literally be known by this name. It is used for reducing overall group taxation exposure. All home country export

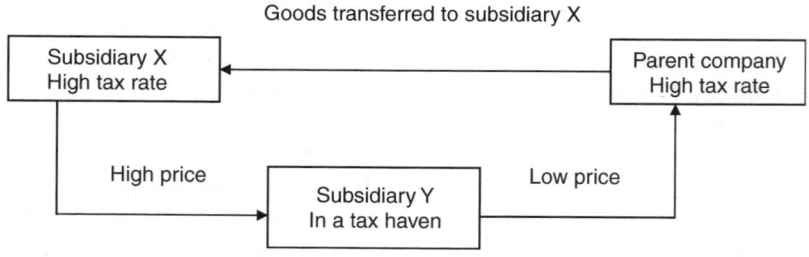

Figure 2.2   Transfer pricing with a tax haven for tax planning purposes

billings are first directed to it in the home country currency. Company Y then re-invoices the relevant affiliates in each affiliate's local currency for the same applicable consignments. By these means, company Y, as the central financial subsidiary can be used to exploit international transactions as shown in this case.

Some multinational enterprises such as drug companies and electronics companies often set up subsidiaries in the tax havens. These companies assign the 'ownership' of their intangible properties such as patents and technical know-how to their subsidiaries, and then claim that a large share of their total profits is 'earned' in the tax havens that enjoy a tax break.

Minimization of worldwide import duties. *Ad valorem* import duties are very high in some countries, especially in those which often suffer from balance-of-payment problems. For them, tariffs are an important instrument for increasing revenues and reducing balance-of-payments problems. To avoid paying high tariffs, a multinational enterprise can lower the price at which goods are transferred to its associated company located in a country in which high import duties are imposed. Low import duties can be associated with high income tax rates. The savings resulting from underinvoicing for customs purposes may be more than offset by higher income tax liabilities because income taxes are, typically, a larger imposition than tariffs.

Minimization of withholding taxes. The term withholding tax refers to income tax deducted at source on interest, dividends and royalties paid by a company to recipients in other countries, or income earned by foreign residents. As a home country cannot tax individuals or companies in foreign host countries, a withholding tax ensures that the governments of the latter gain at least some revenue from such payments. Host governments generally impose a withholding tax of 20% or more on foreign enterprises without establishments in their territories but which receive interest, rental, royalty and other income within their jurisdictions.

Under the terms of bilateral tax treaties, a lower withholding tax rate of 10% or 15% would normally apply to interest and royalty payments between enterprises in a host country and the contracting state. Transfer pricing could then be used to minimize the withholding tax on interest, dividends and royalties. For example, when artificially high prices are set for raw materials or equipment supplied to a subsidiary, the subsidiary may transfer its profits to a parent company by way of its sales price. This leaves less profit in the subsidiary's country, reducing the need to transfer profits to the parent firm through dividends. The subsidiary can thereby exempt part of its profits from the withholding tax.

Maximization of foreign tax credits. To avoid double taxation, many countries employ the foreign tax credit system. A foreign tax credit is a tax credit granted to a parent company in a home country for tax paid in host countries by its subsidiaries. This device, however, can be misused by multinational enterprises to maximize income by way of tax avoidance. A company can use transfer pricing to maximize the benefit of its foreign tax credits by moving assets at spurious prices to the subsidiary to secure full relief in the home country for tax paid in the host country. Three general examples of processes for accomplishing this may be cited.

Example 1. The tax payment already made in the host country is equal to the tax liability awaiting payment in the home country. In this case, under the foreign tax credit system operating between participating countries, the company receives 100% credit and thereby annuls its liability in the home country.

Example 2. The tax payment already made in the host country is half the tax liability awaiting payment in the home country. In this case, the company in the home country receives 100% credit and therefore halves its tax liability in the home country.

Example 3. The tax payment already made in the host country of whatever magnitude contrasts with the nil tax liability in the home country. In this case, the company seeks a device by which it can turn the tax paid in the host country into an asset that otherwise would be lost. It does this by the transfer of assets to the host country thereby generating tax liabilities in the home country and validating a claim for a tax credit.

Chinese practice

In 2004 in excess of 400,000 foreign investment enterprises were believed to be operating in China, but only 280,000 companies were properly registered according to the prevailing regulations. The tax revenue statistics show that 35% to 40% of foreign investment enterprises were in a loss-making position from 1988 to 1993. For 1994 and 1995, the percentage increased to between 50% and 60%. Between 1996 and 2000, 60% to 70% of foreign companies reported losses. Clearly there has been an exponential increase in malpractice.

The Chinese government estimates that 60% of the reported losses by these companies is attributable to transfer pricing manoeuvres. The annual average reported amount lost by these companies together is

RMB 120 billion. This translates into annual losses in taxable revenues of about RMB 30 billion, attributable in large part to the transfer pricing manipulations of foreign investment enterprises, which in this way not only have the effect of eroding the tax revenue of the Chinese government but have a negative impact on the balance of foreign exchange income and expenditure, as well as distorting the image of the China market and its investment environment.

Income tax. The Chinese tax law stipulates that a 30% corporate income tax is collected by the state tax bureaux from foreign investment enterprises and assigned to the central government. In addition, a local surtax of 3% is levied by local tax bureaux as revenue for local governments. Overall these rates are close to the corporate tax rates in China's major trading partners, as shown in Table 2.2, with the singular exception of Hong Kong, which has a low rate of 16%,

Hong Kong has long been the leading source of foreign direct investment in China, originating a high proportion of total foreign direct investment in China during the period 1990 to 2002. Hong Kong adopts a source-based taxation or tax-exemption system whereby corporate taxes are charged only on income sourced in Hong Kong. Profits or revenues repatriated by foreign subsidiaries are exempt from Hong Kong taxation (Chan & Chow, 1998, pp. 38–9). Although many Hong Kong-sourced investments are not actually owned by *bona fide* Hong Kong residents, Hong Kong, given its fairly relaxed approach to international transfer pricing and low tax rates, offers Hong Kong investors the opportunity to adopt structures which divert profits away from their Chinese affiliated companies or subsidiaries (Sun, 1999).

Table 2.2 Income tax rates of some of China's main trading partners

Parent country/region	Income tax rate
Hong Kong	16%
United States	15%–39%
Japan	30%
Taiwan	25.0%
Korea	28%
Malaysia	28%
Singapore	25.5%
United Kingdom	31%
Germany	36%

Source: Ministry of Commerce of the People's Republic of China's website. The website address is http://www.mofcom.gov.cn.

Import duties. Traditionally, customs duty is an important source of revenue for the Chinese central government, but since China joined the World Trade Organization in December 2001, it has cut its customs tariffs on several occasions. These tariff rate cuts were in line with its commitment to reduce average import tariffs to 10% by 2005 and to 9.8% by 2010. The average tariff level of the World Trade Organization members is now about 6%. Compared with other member countries, the customs duties imposed on companies in China are still relatively higher. This may motivate multinational enterprises in China to under-price imports from associated companies to avoid the higher tariffs.

Withholding tax. The Chinese Enterprise Income Law imposes a withholding tax of 10% – or at the rate specified in the tax treaties – on foreign enterprises without establishments in China but which derive passive income such as dividends, interest, royalty, and other income from China.

- Taxes on dividends
  Dividends paid to an overseas parent company from the profits of a foreign investment enterprise are generally exempt from withholding tax, but the dividends cannot be deductible. Likewise, profits repatriated from a branch in China to its overseas head office are also exempt.
- Taxes on interest
  Interest paid on loans to an overseas investment company is deductible provided the interest is charged at a normal market rate. The interest received by the overseas investment company is subject to the basic withholding tax of 20%. However, interest paid by a branch to its overseas head office cannot be deductible. No withholding tax is imposed at all, on the grounds that the head office is the same legal person as the branch.

In 2003, a large foreign investment company's subsidiary in Guangdong province was investigated by the Guangzhou tax bureau for its tax avoidance behaviour. In 2002, the subsidiary's associated companies in China reported constant losses. The subsidiary obtained loans amounting to RMB 2 billion from the Bank of China and then loaned them to its associated companies free of interest. The interest paid on the loans to the Bank by the company was deductible against its taxable income, whilst the associated firms paid no interest to the company, thereby enabling it to avoid tax payments on interest income. The tax bureau adjusted the company's taxable revenue by RMB 0.596 billion and imposed a corresponding corporate income tax charge of RNB 81.49 million.

- Taxes on royalties
  Royalties paid to overseas investment companies for the licensing of trademarks, copyrights, and technical know-how, are deductible provided they are charged at normal market rates. Royalties received by the overseas investment company are subject to a 20% withholding tax. The withholding tax may be reduced to 0% to 10% if the royalties are for the supply of certain advanced proprietary technology under preferential terms. However, royalties paid by a branch to its overseas head office cannot be deductible. Accordingly, there is no withholding tax on royalty transactions between the branch and the overseas head office.

In the year 2002 in Suzhou, a city in Jiangsu province, around 10,000 foreign investment enterprises were operating, 70% (7,000) of them reporting losses. The local customs officials believed that many of them paid excessive royalty fees to their overseas parent companies, thus creating their own financial losses. Since China entered the World Trade Organization in December 2001, its customs officers have enhanced their enforcement efforts with regard to the payment of royalty fees to foreign parent investment companies.

Such enforcement activity when applied retrospectively to royalty payments already made, together with the appropriate due withholding taxes, can lead to controversy. A company can find itself liable for additional customs duties to the local customs offices. In the end this can lead to double taxation. A famous American wholly owned company was established in 1996 in a coastal city. It manufactured and sold sports shoes. The local customs officials found that the company's sales revenues and profit margins were very high, and its costs and expenses were very low, whilst its reported performance rate remained negative. In terms of the license agreement with its parent company, the company had to pay royalty fees to the parent company amounting to 6% of its domestic sales revenue. In 2002, the local customs office imposed customs duties of RMB 2.35 million on the deemed royalty fees, in spite of the fact that the company argued that it had paid the due withholding taxes for the payment of the royalty fees.

- Taxes on management fees
  Overhead expenses paid to overseas investment companies cannot be deductible. Accordingly, no withholding tax is charged on the

payment of management expenses. However, if the head office can substantiate the allocation of its administrative expenses to the Chinese branch with a verification report from a certified public accountant, then the overhead expenses can be deductible.

China has already concluded more than 80 tax treaties with other countries on income and capital. Under the terms of these bilateral tax treaties, the withholding tax rate is reduced to 10% or less. Likewise, the 10% reduced withholding tax rate also applies to interest and royalty income earned by foreign investors if the payer of such income is located in China in Special Economic Zones, Coastal Open Cities, Coastal Open Economic Zones, Designated Provincial Capitals, Economic and Technological Development Zones, Shanghai Pudong New Areas, and Tax Bonded Areas. In 1999, the state administration of taxation issued a circular that reduced the withholding tax rate on all China sourced income received by overseas entities to 10%. This reduced withholding tax rate has been effective since 1 January 2000 (Cho, 1998; Mo, 2003).

Foreign Tax Credits. Foreign investment enterprises with their head offices in China are generally taxed on their worldwide income. Meanwhile, the Chinese tax law allows foreign investment enterprises to avoid double taxation of their foreign-sourced income by applying for a foreign tax credit, that is, foreign income tax paid abroad in respect of foreign-sourced income can be claimed against the Chinese tax payable in respect of the same income. Moreover, an unused foreign tax credit can be carried forward for not more than five years. Foreign tax credits have some tax planning implications for multinational companies in China.

Summary

Taxation and other charges on commercial transactions between associated companies can be a major cost in a competitive market. Multinational enterprises can use their structural forms and internal organization to transfer assets from one member of the group to another across national boundaries and different tax jurisdictions to minimize their fiscal obligations by the adroit pricing of those assets in relation to the prevailing tax levels of the destination country. Elaborate and ostensibly legal manoeuvres can be adopted for the purpose. China's taxation levels have been a magnet for such practices on a vast scale, arousing the attention of the tax authorities and the implementation of corrective measures.

Part II
Mechanics of Audit

3
Transfer Pricing Rules of Trading Partners

Introduction

With the growth of the global economy, many national governments in the face of the magnitude of the issue of transfer pricing, have enacted legislation for the operation of a regulatory service under their tax authorities. At varying levels of comprehensiveness, the legislation specifies the detailed means by which the authorities intend to prevent abuses of transfer pricing and to deal with them when they occur. Consequently, the content of national legislation lays down the standards expected of good practice, the treatment to be adopted for the correction of failure to follow them, and the penalties that may be applied in the event of convicted malpractice.

The main differences between national codes for the control of transfer pricing vary with respect to the conceptualization of an offence, the methods by which a proven offence may be rectified, the processes and requirements expected of good practice, and the penalties to be imposed for recalcitrance.

Some of the most rigorous tax authorities in the world are the seven predominant industrial economies – Canada, France, Germany, Italy, Japan, the United Kingdom, and the United States. These governments have enacted transfer pricing legislation and have issued guidelines to safeguard their national interests. The United States leads the way in this regard. It has enacted the toughest and perhaps the most comprehensive transfer pricing rules and regulations in the world.

An important development over the subject of protection from transfer pricing abuse was a report entitled *Transfer Pricing and Multinational Enterprises* released by the Organization for Economic Cooperation and Development (OECD) Committee on Fiscal Affairs in 1979, which was influenced by the experience and regulatory framework previously developed by the United States. Later reports issued by the OECD addressed related issues, in particular in *Transfer Pricing and Multinational Enterprises – Three Taxation Issues* (1984) and *Thin Capitalization* (1987). In 1995, the OECD adopted major amendments to the 1979 Report and issued *Transfer Pricing Guidelines for Multinational Enterprises and Tax Administrations*.

Transfer pricing methods

Many methods are used by companies for arriving at prices charged, and by tax authorities when they impose an audit for adjusting those prices on its being considered justifiable. The status and usefulness of each derive from its ability to serve the preferred standard of pricing, known as the arm's length principle.

The arm's length principle. China's policy, in common with that of national governments in general, is to require that transactions between associated enterprises are priced on an open market basis, as if between unrelated parties.

Six prominently used methods. The following six methods are the most commonly found in practice. They form two sub-groups. The first three are transaction or price-based in nature, the second three are profit-based in nature. By and large the first three are favoured by tax authorities.

The comparable uncontrolled price method (CUP). The comparable uncontrolled price method compares the price charged for property or services transferred in a controlled transaction to the price charged for property or services transferred in a comparable uncontrolled transaction in comparable circumstances. The term 'controlled' in this context refers to pricing agreed by the contracting parties for subjective reasons, as opposed to open market pricing.

The resale price method (RP). The resale price method determines an arm's length price for transactions between associated enterprises by comparing the gross margin earned on a controlled transaction with the gross margin earned in similar uncontrolled transactions. The resale price method begins with the price at which a product, purchased from an associated enterprise, is resold to an independent enterprise. This resale price is then reduced by an appropriate resale price margin to determine the arm's length cost of the product payable by the associated supplier.

The cost plus method (CPL). The cost plus method begins with the costs incurred by the supplier for making the product or performing the service. A cost plus mark up is then added to the cost – for an appropriate profit earned in the light of functions performed and the market conditions – to determine the arm's length price to charge the associated purchaser.

The profit split method (PS). The profit split method calculates an arm's length net profit for each of the associated enterprises by determining the combined profit attributable to the associated enterprises in the controlled transaction, and then splitting that profit according to the relative economic value of the contribution that each enterprise made to that transaction.

The comparable profit method (CP). The comparable profit method prices a transaction by using objective measures of profitability derived from the records of uncontrolled taxpayers that engage in similar business activities under similar circumstances. The comparable profit method deals with income, whereas the transactional net profit margin method deals with pricing.

Transactional net margin method (TNM). The transactional net margin method determines an arm's length profit by comparing the net profit margin obtained by an associated enterprise with that obtained by a comparable independent firm. The United States' regulations stipulate the use of the comparable profit method as a replacement for the transactional net profit margin method.

OECD transfer pricing guidelines

Acceptable pricing methods. The basic principle permeating the OECD Guidelines is that an arm's length price should be used in all intercompany cross-border transactions. Several pricing methods have been developed for calculating the arm's length price. The OECD Guidelines prescribe that the arm's length price is determined by using one or more of the price-based methods. Table 3.1 lists transfer pricing methods accepted by the OECD Guidelines and the methods variously adopted by the 30 OECD countries.

A non-arm's length approach: Global Formulary Apportionment. The global formulary apportionment method allocates the global profits of a multinational group on a consolidated basis among its associated enterprises in different countries, using a pre-set formula. The OECD Guidelines mentions this particular method as an adjunct to the normally used methods cited above, recognizing that some companies choose to use it, but rejecting it as an acceptable and recommendable method.

Table 3.1 Acceptable transfer pricing methods

Method	CUP	RP	CPL	PS	CP	TNM
OECD	Yes	Yes	Yes	Yes	No	Yes
Australia	Yes	Yes	Yes	Yes	No	Yes
Austria	Yes	Yes	Yes	Yes	No	Yes
Belgium	Yes	Yes	Yes	Yes	No	Yes
Canada	Yes	Yes	Yes	Yes	No	Yes
Czech Republic	Yes	Yes	Yes	Yes	No	Yes
Denmark	Yes	Yes	Yes	Yes	No	Yes
Finland	Yes	Yes	Yes	Yes	No	Yes
France	Yes	Yes	Yes	Yes	No	Yes
Germany	Yes	Yes	Yes	Yes	No	Yes
Greece	Unclear	Unclear	Unclear	Unclear	Unclear	Unclear
Hungary	Yes	Yes	Yes	Yes	No	Yes
Iceland	Unclear	Unclear	Unclear	Unclear	Unclear	Unclear
Ireland	Yes	Yes	Yes	Yes	No	Yes
Italy	Yes	Yes	Yes	Yes	Yes	No
Japan	Yes	Yes	Yes	Yes	No	Yes
Korea	Yes	Yes	Yes	Yes	No	Yes
Luxembourg	Yes	Yes	Yes	Yes	No	Yes
Mexico	Yes	Yes	Yes	Yes	No	Yes
Netherlands	Yes	Yes	Yes	Yes	No	Yes
New Zealand	Yes	Yes	Yes	Yes	Yes	No
Norway	Yes	Yes	Yes	Yes	No	Yes
Poland	Yes	Yes	Yes	Yes	No	Yes
Portugal	Yes	Yes	Yes	Yes	No	Yes
Slovakia	Yes	Yes	Yes	Yes	No	Yes
Spain	Yes	Yes	Yes	Yes	No	Yes
Sweden	Yes	Yes	Yes	Yes	No	Yes
Switzerland	Yes	Yes	Yes	Yes	No	Yes
Turkey	Unclear	Unclear	Unclear	Unclear	Unclear	Unclear
United Kingdom	Yes	Yes	Yes	Yes	No	Yes
United States	Yes	Yes	Yes	Yes	Yes	No

Sources: Ernst and Young (2004b); Deloitte (2006).

Documentation and penalties. With regard to documentation requirements, the OECD Guidelines suggest a flexible approach, recommending the maintenance of a level and detail of documentation that allow the verification of compliance while not burdening firms with excessive time and cost demands. For example, the Guidelines suggest that each taxpayer should try to determine transfer pricing 'in accordance with the arm's length principle, based upon information reasonably available at the time of the determination'. By definition, the information needed will vary depending upon the facts and circumstances of the case.

As with documentation requirements, the OECD Guidelines do not suggest specific penalties but recommend that each country should set penalties of such a kind that 'tax underpayments and other types of non-compliance are more costly than compliance' (OECD, 1995, p. IV-7).

Advance pricing agreement. The 1995 OECD Guidelines proposed advance pricing arrangements as one of several administrative approaches for resolving transfer pricing disputes. The OECD Guidelines define an advance pricing agreement as an arrangement that determines, in advance of controlled transactions, an appropriate set of criteria for the determination of the transfer pricing for those transactions over a fixed period of time (OECD, 1995, p. G-1). These criteria would typically include the method adopted for arriving at prices, comparable data related to the transaction, appropriate adjustments that could be made to them, and critical assumptions about future events bearing on the company's commercial activities.

United States

Over the past decades, the United States has regularly revised its transfer pricing regulations and initiated new rules to strengthen the power of the Internal Revenue Service to control transfer pricing practices. Sections 482, 6038A, 6038C, and 6062(e)–(h) of the Internal Revenue Code, bulwarked by many subsequent regulations and rulings, authorize the Internal Revenue Service to allocate income or deductions among related companies to prevent tax evasion, reflecting the justifiable income of each company.

As stated in Section 482 of the 1954 Internal Revenue Code: 'In any case of two or more organizations, trades, or businesses (whether or not incorporated, whether or not organized in the United States, and whether or not affiliated) owned or controlled directly or indirectly by the same interests, the Secretary or his delegate may distribute, apportion, or allocate gross income, deductions, credits, or allowances between or among such organizations, trades, or businesses, if he determines that such distribution, apportionment, or allocation is necessary in order to prevent the evasion of taxes or clearly to reflect the income of any such organizations, trades, or businesses'.

Acceptable pricing methods. The most recent version of the United States regulations under Section 482 released in 1994 adopts the comparable uncontrolled price method, the resale price method, and the cost-plus method. As for the profit-based methods, the only difference from the OECD approach is that the United States regulations stipulate the use of the comparable profit method as a replacement for the transactional net profit margin method, and allow for the use of the profit split method.

Burden of proof. According to the United States regulations, the allocation of income between related parties made by the Internal Revenue Service will be sustained by the courts, unless the taxpayer can establish that the allocation is 'arbitrary, capricious or unreasonable'. In this regard, the burden of proof lies squarely with the taxpayer who must prove that his prices are charged at arm's length.

Documentation and penalties. The United States Internal Revenue Service adopts a demanding approach to documentation requirements for multinational enterprises. Documentation should be contemporaneous and include all relevant information. The level of detail, and the types of documentation required, are often considered onerous by multinational enterprises in terms of their exhaustiveness and quantity. The Internal Revenue Service has stated that the objective of the United States penalty regime is to encourage taxpayers to make reasonable efforts to determine and document the arm's length character of their intercompany transfer prices. Therefore, a company can avoid a detailed transfer pricing audit and the risk of transfer pricing penalties by preparing and maintaining contemporaneous documentation to establish that its selection and application of a pricing method provided the most accurate measure of an arm's length result.

A complex and tough transfer pricing penalty regime is in place. Section 6662 imposes transactional and net adjustment penalties for misstatements. These penalties are not deductible in determining gross income. Two penalty levels of 20% and 40% may be imposed.

Advance pricing agreement. In 1991, the United States Internal Revenue Service introduced the advance pricing agreement procedures. As stated in IRS Rev Proc 96-53 of Section 482, an advance pricing agreement is defined as 'an agreement between the Internal Revenue Service and the taxpayer on the transfer pricing methodology to be applied to any apportionment or location of income, deductions, credits, or allowances between or among two or more organizations, trades, or businesses owned or controlled, directly or indirectly, by the same interests'.

The United States regulations contain a more detailed and formalized advance pricing agreement programme – with specific and detailed disclosure procedures and restrictions – than those promulgated by any other country which follows the OECD approach to the matter. For instance, to obtain an advance pricing agreement, the taxpayer must submit detailed information along with a $5,000 user fee. Once the advance pricing agreement is approved, the taxpayer is obligated to maintain sufficient books and records to enable the Internal Revenue Service to verify the taxpayer's compliance with the advance pricing agreement. In addition, the taxpayer must submit an annual report to the Internal Revenue Service describing advance pricing agreement activities. Both unilateral and bilateral agreements may be contracted.

Canada

Following a review over three years, in September 1999 the Canadian government published *Information Circular 87-2R* on the subject of the law on transfer pricing and its administration. Canadian policy is wedded to the arm's length principle but implicit in its regulatory provisions is a recognition of the subjective nature of the principle and the difficulties that applying it – and the enforcement of its use – can generate in practice. Canada did not thereby identify any preferred pricing methods and avoided any attempt to promulgate exhaustive provisions to cover every conceivable eventuality. At the same time the government has increased the number of staff devoted to the detection and resolution of transfer pricing irregularities.

Companies must state that they have maintained contemporaneous documentation for transactions with overseas associates if the total value of their transactions exceeds $1 million. For each transaction the documentation must be comprehensive, including details of the goods, services and finances involved, the parties to the transaction, the risks undertaken by each, the terms and conditions governing the transaction, and the factors determining the transfer price.

Against a background of failure to deter transfer pricing abuses by successful court action, the government introduced a penalty regime that was intended to encourage multinational companies to comply with the contemporaneous documentation requirements or to seek an advance pricing agreement under *Circular 94-4R* (March 2001) – which provides for unilateral, bilateral, and multilateral agreements. Both the documentation requirements and other costs for an advance pricing agreement, however, present themselves to companies as expensive alternatives to the commonly taken course of transfer pricing manoeuvres that run the risk of challenge and court action.

The rules provide for the imposition of penalties for proven wilful non-compliance, equaling 10% of the excess of the amount by which a company's taxable income has been reduced by a transfer pricing manoeuvre, over the lesser of $5 million or 10% of the taxpayer's gross income. This imposition can even be applied in a year when the company in question has no taxable income for that year.

To avoid the penalty a taxpayer must be able to show that reasonable efforts had been made to prepare records and documents as required, and is able to present the reasoning used to determine the particular price under review before the final tax filing date.

On the whole Canada has been a champion of price related methods, in line with OECD preferences, the cost plus method in certain circumstances being also admissible. The hierarchy of methods as preferred remains, therefore, the transaction-based methods, followed by the profit split method, and finally the comparable profit method.

France

Provisions for transfer pricing are made under the French Tax Administration's *General Tax Code, Article 57* and *Tax Procedure Book, Articles L13B* and *L188A*. Regulations and rulings are made in the *Administrative Doctrine on Article 57* and *on Article L13B*. A preference for transaction-based methods for transfer pricing is stated, with a hierarchy of specific credibility being attributed to the comparable uncontrolled price, resale price, cost plus, profit split, and transaction net margin methods. Advance pricing agreements became available from September 1999 on a bilateral basis with tax treaty countries which have determined a mutual agreement procedure. Unilateral agreements since then have been subject to development on an informal basis.

Tax reforms introduced in 1996 provided for obligatory documentation and enlarged the powers of the tax authorities to conduct transfer pricing audits. The tax authority has a right under the law to obtain details of the relations between a French company and its foreign associates, the nature of the relationships involved, the activities undertaken by the associate, the methods used to determine transfer prices for transactions between them, and details of the tax regime governing the business of the associate if the French company owns more than 50% of its shares or owns it as a subsidiary.

Simultaneously with these stronger enforcement moves, the government has mounted the expectation that the adoption of the advance price agreement with its required annual report will become a widespread feature of company policy with respect to transfer pricing. The French government hopes thereby to induce a more cooperative relationship between the company and the tax authority. Fixed fines or penalties between 40% and 80% of the additional tax assessed can be imposed on companies found to be guilty of fraud.

By 1999 nearly 80% of French multinational companies reported that a transfer pricing investigation had been undertaken into at least one of their associate companies either in France or abroad – a rate greatly in excess of that of previous years. A new category of specially trained staff has been introduced specifically to share tax information with the tax authorities of other countries. Other highly trained staff members working with tax inspectors are authorized to examine a company's computer system for the direct collection of required information.

Germany

Under the Federal Ministry of Finance, policy over transfer pricing has been expressed in a number of publications during the last twenty years. These include

– *Corporate Income Tax Act* and *Foreign Transactions Tax Act*
– Administration Principles, *Circular of the Federal Ministry of Finance,* 23 February 1983, *Federal Gazette 1,* 1983
– Principles for the Review of Income Determination through Cost Allocation Agreements Among Internationally Related Parties, *Circular of the Federal Ministry of Finance,* 30 December 1999; *Cost Allocation Circular, Federal Gazette 1,* 1999
– Administrative Principles Relating to the Examination of Apportionment of Income in the Case of Permanent Establishments of Internationally Operating Enterprises, 24 December 1999; *Permanent Establishment Circular, Federal Gazette 1,* 1999
– *Corporate Income Tax Directive,* Section 36a
– *Transfer Pricing Documentation Law,* 17 October 2003.

In common with France, Germany favours the employment of transaction-based methods for the determination of transfer pricing, specifically naming the comparable uncontrolled price, resale price, and cost plus as the preferred methods, with the profit split method as a last resort.

Previously, specified detailed documentation was not imposed on companies, although an obligation to be cooperative with the tax authorities was regarded as incumbent on them under the *General Tax Act*, Section 90, as was the duty to be prudent and diligent over business documentation, consistent with the expectations of good management practice. The law of 2003, however, in reflecting the growing international concern over the scale of transfer pricing abuse, made it compulsory for companies engaged in cross-border transactions to maintain full documentation and include in it evidence to show that an arm's length principle had been used to determine prices. Failure to do so can result in an adjustment of the taxable income and can carry substantial fines or minimum penalties of between 5% and 10% of the additional tax due as a result of an adjustment.

An increasing interest in international transactions has been shown by the tax authorities. They expect a full disclosure of information about them and a willingness to make documents generated outside of Germany available for inspection. Advance pricing agreements of a bilateral nature are available but are not enjoined on companies.

Italy

The Ministry of Finance administers the law for transfer pricing under *Presidential Decree n.917, Article 76(5)* and *Article 9 (3) (4)*, and *Presidential Decree n.660, Article 32, Legislative Decrees n.471, Article 1*, and *74/2000*. *Circular Letters 32/9/2267* of 22 September 1980, and *42/12/1587* of 12 December 1981 contained regulations and rulings.

In recent years Italy has increased its vigilance over transfer pricing abuse. With additional specialist staff at their disposal, the tax authorities have increased their audit activity in the case of companies in the country operating with cross-border transactions.

The documentation requirements have moved in common with those required in France and Germany, in line with OECD Guidelines. Details of all transactions should include full justification for the pricing methods chosen and any departure from an arm's length principle, and full details of all associates involved in such transactions.

The criminal law provisions of 2000 allow for penalties for tax fraud in addition to the application of the long standing penalties for tax underpayments. For taxable income adjustment purposes, transaction-based methods are preferred to profit-based methods. Comparable uncontrolled price, resale price, cost plus, profit split, comparable profit, economic sector gross margin, and invested capital profitability methods are specifically mentioned.

Japan

The National Tax Administration operates under the *Special Taxation Measures Law, Article 66-4*, and has the benefit of *Enforcement Order 39-12, Circular 66-4-(1)-1 to 66-4-(7)2*, and the *Administrative Guideline* of 1 June 2001 and its partial revision of 20 June 2002. Japan generally follows the OECD Guidelines. A tax reform law introduced in 2003 requires full documentation for cross-border transactions, including details of the information and methods used to determine arm's length prices.

Japan promulgated its first rules for transfer pricing in 1986. Subsequent government documents have been concerned to clarify issues and define terms – notably the factors to be taken into consideration when determining an arm's length price, but also the meaning of a comparable transaction, and the nature and value of various pricing methods. Transaction-based methods are preferred to profit-based methods. Comparable uncontrolled price, resale price, cost plus, and profit split are specified.

Unilateral and bilateral advance pricing agreements are provided for since 2001, the latter being preferred. Graduated penalties may be imposed according to the magnitude of the adjusted additional tax due and whether fraudulent conduct had been involved.

United Kingdom

The Inland Revenue operates under Schedule 28AA, *Income and Corporation Taxes Act* of 1988, and Section 12B of the *Taxes Management Act* of 1970, with the benefit of Guidance Notes in *Tax Bulletins 37* and *38*. Since 1999, new rules govern transfer pricing practice. Companies come under the United Kingdom's general practice of self-assessment. Documentation is not routinely required with returns. It is however expected to be available and consistent with normal accounting practice and is required as specified under an advance pricing agreement. It is necessary for defending an audit. It should include details of the method used to determine an arm's length price, information regarding a company's associates, full details of the transactions themselves, and the processes by which they took place.

Companies are obligated under the law to ascertain the arm's length pricing nature of transactions conducted with overseas associates. The United Kingdom's position over pricing method is cast in terms of the most reasonable method, but transaction-based methods are explicitly preferred to profit-based methods. The comparable uncontrolled price, resale price, cost plus, profit split, and transaction net margin methods are specified. Failing to comply with the legislation can attract a penalty of 100% of the additional tax due as a result of an adjustment. A fine of up to 3,000 pounds sterling may be imposed for failure to keep proper records, and a fine of up to 10,000 pounds sterling if misleading or false information is submitted as part of an application for an advance pricing agreement.

Summary

Transfer pricing is an important international tax issue. An international transfer pricing transaction normally takes place between two or more companies, and involves two or more tax jurisdictions. Therefore, the transfer price adopted by a multinational company has a direct bearing on the profit of a company and has tax implications for more than one national tax jurisdiction.

The transfer pricing approaches and methods accepted by a company's tax jurisdiction in its home country may not be in agreement with those of the tax administration in an overseas host country. In such a case, double taxation can ensue if a transaction is treated at a different transfer price by two incompatible national tax authorities.

To reduce the risk of double taxation, it is important for a multinational firm with subsidiaries operating in foreign countries to notice the regulatory differences on transfer pricing between those of its home country and those of foreign host countries. This chapter has reviewed OECD Guidelines and the transfer pricing regulations of seven prominent industrial countries, known popularly as the G7 – Canada, France, Germany, Italy, Japan, the United Kingdom, and the United States – which meet to discuss international trade from time to time. These countries have built the most rigorous tax regimes in the world. Their tax laws have a significant bearing on the transfer pricing practices of Chinese subsidiaries of multinational enterprises.

4
China's Transfer Pricing Rules

Introduction

China's transfer pricing legislation was first enacted in 1991. The same transfer pricing rules have also been incorporated into the tax collection law since 1992, effectively broadening the applicable scope of transfer pricing to all taxes in China. Several tax rules and circulars have been announced since then to assist with their implementation. To reinforce the regulatory framework, the State Administration of Taxation issued specific implementing measures between 1992 and 2005. From time to time, the State Administration of Taxation has also issued notices urging local tax authorities to strengthen transfer pricing enforcement.

At present, the major transfer pricing regulations in China consist of the following.

- *The Income Tax Law of the People's Republic of China for Enterprises with Foreign Investment and Foreign Enterprises* (effective 1 July 1991) (Income Tax Law for Foreign Investment Enterprises and Foreign Enterprises), and *Detailed Rules for Implementation of the Income Tax Law of the People's Republic of China for Enterprises with Foreign Investment and Foreign Enterprises* (effective 1 July 1991) (Detailed Rules)
- *Tax Administration Rules for Business Transactions between Associated Enterprises* (effective 1 January 1993)
- *Tax Administration Rules and Procedures for Transactions between Related Parties* (effective 23 April 1998) (State Administration of Taxation Circular No. 59)
- *The Law of the People's Republic of China Concerning Tax Collection and Administration* (amended and effective 1 May 2001) (Tax Collection

Law), and its detailed *Implementing Rules* (amended and effective 15 October 2002) (Tax Collection Implementing Rules)
- *The Rules for Administration of Business Transactions between Affiliated Enterprises* (For Trial Implementation) (amended 22 October 2004) (Transfer Pricing Rules)
- *Implementation Rules for Advance Pricing Arrangements for Transactions between Related Parties* (effective 3 September 2004)
- *Provisional Measures for PRC Residents (Nationals) to Apply for Tax Mutual Consultation Process* (effective 1 July 2005)
- *Notice of the State Administration of Taxation on the Issue of Capital Intensity Adjustments in Transfer Pricing Related Tax Administration* (Guo Shui Fa [2005] No. 745; effective 28 July 2005).

Current transfer pricing rules

China is a late-comer to the transfer pricing arena, having launched a policy of economic intercourse with the rest of the world only as late as 1979. In the early years of this policy, transfer pricing was not a significant concern for the Chinese government because its energies were mainly focused on attracting foreign direct investments and also because China lacked an institutional and organizational framework to deal with the practical issues involved.

Since then, however, China's enormous market potential and cheap labour costs, along with a series of preferential tax policies for foreign investors, have combined to encourage large numbers of foreign investment enterprises to embark on investment opportunities in China. The wide range of related party transactions typically engaged in by foreign investment enterprises with overseas affiliated companies, together with the fact that variably over half of foreign investment enterprises have been reporting operating losses up to 2004, have in turn combined to imply that the potential for transfer pricing manipulations in China has been immense. In 1981 and 1982, the Joint Venture Income Law and Foreign Enterprise Income Tax Law were enacted, yet neither of these two laws mentioned the transfer pricing issue.

Since the early 1990s, however, the Chinese government has noted the phenomenon and has taken steps to combat tax avoidance by means of transfer pricing abuses by foreign investment enterprises in China. In November 1990, the State Administration of Taxation issued a set of provisional rules regarding the administration of taxation for transactions between foreign investment enterprises and their associated enterprises.

These rules set out general guidelines for the transfer prices of these transactions and provided the basis for subsequent legislation.

The Chinese transfer pricing legislation was first introduced in 1991 by the National People's Congress under the *Income Tax Law of the People's Republic of China for Enterprises with Foreign Investment and Foreign Enterprises* (Tax Law). The transfer pricing legislation – Article 13 of the Tax Law – adopts the arm's length principle, which stipulates that 'the payment or receipt of charges or fees in business transactions between an enterprise with foreign investment, or an establishment or a place set up in China by a foreign enterprise to engage in production or business operations, and its associated enterprises, shall be made in the same manner as the payment or receipt of charges or fees in business transactions between independent enterprises. Where the payment or receipt of charges or fees is not made in the same manner as in business transactions between independent enterprises and results in a reduction of income tax, the tax authorities shall have the right to make reasonable adjustments.'

Article 13 of the Tax Law is further supplemented by Articles 52 to 58 of the *Detailed Implementing Rules of the Tax Law*. The Tax Law has been in force since 1 July 1991, and the Implementing Rules since 30 June 1991.

In 1992, The State Administration of Taxation released a circular entitled *Tax Administration Rules for Business Transactions between Associated Enterprises* (effective 1 January 1993). This circular clarifies the criteria for the identification of associated enterprises, defines the procedures for the yearly reporting of business transactions with related parties, and specifies the extent of an enterprise's responsibility to provide evidence that it has conducted international transactions according to the law.

On 23 April 1998, the State Administration of Taxation issued comprehensive transfer pricing regulations entitled *Tax Administration Rules and Procedures for Transactions between Related Parties* (State Administration of Taxation Circular No. 59). This Circular contains 52 articles and 12 chapters which standardize transfer pricing examination and audit procedures, including the selection of companies for tax examination, desk audits, field audits, the application of adjustment methods, evidence collection, tax collection, applications for appeal, and the internal co-ordination between local tax bureaux and the State Administration of Taxation. These regulations were reflected and confirmed in the *Tax Administration Law* (2001) and its *Detailed Implementation Rules* (2002).

On 9 June 2004, the State Administration of Taxation issued a notice in respect of its increasing efforts to tackle tax avoidance schemes entered into between the related parties of multinational companies. This notice requires the local tax authorities to adopt various measures to enhance their anti-tax avoidance performance.

The State Administration of Taxation released another notice, coming into effect on 28 July 2005, on the issue of capital intensity adjustments in transfer pricing related to tax administration (*Circular 745*). The notice states that 'when comparing the profit levels of the company under investigation and the comparable companies, if differences exist between the company under investigation and the comparable companies in the utilization of operating capital such as accounts receivable, accounts payable, and inventory, adjustments should be made to account for the impact of the utilized operating capital on profit levels in order to obtain economically more reliable operating profits, and to enhance the comparability of the profit levels of the comparable companies.' The issue of *Circular 745* illustrates the State Administration of Taxation's increasing efforts to understand and cope with the more sophisticated elements of transfer pricing in China and to deter malpractice.

China has already conducted tax treaties with more than 80 countries and regions. These treaties provide for mutual agreement procedures for resolving cross-border, tax-related disputes. On 7 July 2005, the State Administration of Taxation issued a new set of rules (Guo Shui Fa [2005] No. 115) to provide guidance for implementing mutual agreement procedures in China. These rules apply to Chinese nationals and residents, including foreign investment enterprises established and registered in the country.

China's transfer pricing regime

Associated enterprises. The Chinese transfer pricing rules only apply to transactions that are conducted between or among related parties or controlled parties. An associated enterprise is defined in Article 52 of the *Detailed Implementing Rules of the Tax Law* as an enterprise having one of the following relationships with the taxpayer.

- Direct or indirect ownership or control of capital, business operations, purchasing, and selling
- Common ownership or control, directly or indirectly, by a third party;
- Any other associations which generate mutual benefits.

Transfer pricing methods. The Chinese transfer pricing regulations endorse and support the arm's length principle. According to the rules, tangible asset prices must have a transaction basis, using one of three specified methods as follows, but with an allowance for the use of a fourth alternative if conditions and circumstances can justify its use.

- the comparable uncontrolled price method
- the resale price method
- the cost plus method
- any other reasonable method.

For transactions involving the intercompany provision of services, loans, and the transfer of other assets, no particular methods are stipulated for determining their arm's length pricing. Arm's length prices under such circumstances are broadly referred to as any payments or receipts that a third party would agree to for the same kind of transaction.

Required documentation. The issue of formally required compulsory contemporaneous transfer pricing documentation is expected to be made by China in the near future. At present, the transfer pricing regulations do not yet specifically require taxpayers to maintain contemporaneous documentation. Under *Circular 143*, taxpayers are required to provide the following information upon request.

- Facts relating to transactions with related enterprises and third parties, including sales and purchases, financing, the provision of labour services, assignments of tangible and intangible assets, and the provision of rights to use tangible and intangible assets
- Facts on elements that may contribute to the prices, such as the amount, place, form, payment method of a transaction, and other relevant materials used for determining the transaction prices charged or paid, or the basis for making such charges or payments
- Other relevant materials for determining transaction prices or the basis for them.

Burden of proof. In China, the burden of proof regarding the arm's length price in related party transactions rests with the taxpayer. The tax authorities are not required to prove that the taxpayer intended to avoid Chinese tax. When the tax authorities suspect that a foreign investment enterprise's income has been reduced as a result of non-arm's length pricing, the tax authorities will require the foreign investment enterprise to provide relevant information regarding transfer pricing.

Penalties. For the late filing of the related party transactions declaration, no specific transfer pricing penalties have yet been made explicit, except for the penalty of from RMB 2,000 to RMB 10,000. The transfer pricing adjustments made subsequent to an audit, however, can be punitive.

Advance pricing agreements. Article 48 of *Circular 59* has introduced the concept of the advance pricing arrangement. To save transfer pricing audit costs, a foreign investment enterprise is allowed to provide relevant information and fill out the application form for using the advanced pricing method. After a review of the information and documents, the tax authority may sign an advance pricing agreement with the enterprise and then supervise its implementation. In 2004, the document *Implementation Rules for Advance Pricing Arrangements for Transactions between Related Parties* was issued (effective from 3 September 2004), setting out detailed guidelines on advance pricing arrangement procedures. According to the rules, a complete advance pricing arrangement process will consist of the following steps – pre-filing, a formal application, a review and evaluation, negotiations and drafting of the advance pricing agreement, signing the advance pricing agreement, and the execution and monitoring of the agreement in practice. This process may take about 11 months to be completed. Agreements should be valid for two to four years following the year of application and may be renewable. With the approval of the tax authority, an advance pricing arrangement may be retroactively applicable to the year of application.

Compared with the transfer pricing regulations of developed economies, the Chinese transfer pricing legislation is considered rudimentary. Unlike other countries' transfer pricing regulations which focus on corporate income tax, the Chinese transfer pricing regulations might be applicable not only to income tax, but also to other taxes, such as value-added tax, consumption tax, and business tax. Additionally, not only cross-border transactions but also domestic transactions conducted between associated enterprises are targets for transfer pricing examination – although in practice it appears that the Chinese transfer pricing audits have focused mainly on cross-border transactions.

Under China's transfer pricing rules, the relationship test of associated parties is far reaching. Two companies may be considered as associated enterprises by the Chinese tax authorities that in other national tax jurisdictions would not be considered related. Therefore, dealings between seemingly unrelated parties in the view of some foreign jurisdictions can be caught out by the Chinese rules. As such, taxpayers in China are under an excessive burden to confirm that the involved price is of arm's length in nature. Finally, in most cases in China, transfer pricing only applies to foreign investment enterprises (De Souza, 2003).

Summary

This chapter has outlined the legislative and administrative framework in China for the regulation of transfer pricing, the detection of fraudulent pricing, and the management of discovered cases of malpractice. In the previous chapter, Chapter 3, similar data were given for the OECD, the United States, and the prominent member countries of the OECD. In Tables 4.1 to 4.9 below, the key transfer pricing policy and practice data of these foreign countries are variously tabulated and summarized for comparative purposes with those of China (Ernst and Young, 2004b; Deloitte, 2006).

Table 4.1 Tax authority and tax law

OECD	Not applicable
China	State Administration of Taxation (SAT); Article 36 of the *Tax Collection and Administration Law* (Tax Collection Law); Article 13 of the PRC *Income Tax Law for Foreign-Invested Enterprises and Foreign Enterprises* and its *Detailed Rules for Implementation*, Articles 52–58
Canada	Canada Revenue Agency (CRA); Canadian *Income Tax Act* Section 247
France	French Tax Administration; *General Tax Code* Articles 57, Article 238A and 209B. *Tax Procedure Book* Article L.13B. *Supreme Tax Court Case Law on Abnormal Act of Management*
Germany	Federal Ministry of Finance; Section 8 para. 3 *Corporate Income Tax Act*; Section 1 *Foreign Transactions Act*; Section 90 para. 3 and Section 162 para. 3 and 4 *General Tax Code. Decree Law on the Manner, Content and Extent of Documentation* in the sense of Section 90 para. 3 of the *General Tax Code* of 28 October 2003
Italy	Ministry of Finance; Article 110 (7) of *Presidential Decree* n. 917/1986. Article 11 – bis (2) of *Legislative Decree* n. 466/1997
Japan	National Tax Administration; *Special Taxation Measures Law*; Article 66-4
United Kingdom	Inland Revenue; Section 770 and Schedule 28AA, *Income and Corporate Taxes Act* of 1988 (ICTA). Mutual agreement procedure covered in Section 815 AA ICTA and *European Union Arbitration Convention* in Section 815B. Advance pricing agreements covered in Section 85-87 *Finance Act* of 1999
United States	Internal Revenue Service (IRS). *Internal Revenue Code* § 482

Table 4.2 Regulations, rules and guidelines

OECD	*Transfer Pricing Guidelines for Multinational Enterprises and Tax Administrations*
China	*Taxation Administration Rules for Business Transactions between Associated Enterprises* (Guo Shui Fa [1998] No. 59) and *Amended Taxation Administration Rules for Business Transactions between Associated Enterprises* (Guo Shui Fa [2004] No. 143)
Canada	CRA *Information Circular 87-2R*
France	Administrative Doctrine on Articles 57 and 238A of the *French Tax Code*, and Article L13B of the *French Procedure Code*
Germany	*Administration Principles*, Circular of the Federal Ministry of Finance. *Principles for the Review of Income Determination through Cost Allocation Agreements among Internationally Related Parties*, Circular of the Federal Ministry of Finance. *Administrative Principles relating to the Examination of Apportionment of Income in the Case of Permanent Establishments of Internationally Operating Enterprises.* *Principles for the Examination of Allocation of Expenses between Internationally Affiliated Enterprises for the Cross-border Secondment of Employees*, Circular of the Federal Ministry of Finance
Italy	*Circular Letters* nos. *32/9/2267, 42/12/1587* and *271/E/1059*; *Circular Letters* nos. *141/E/862270, 98/E/107570* and *148E/139500*
Japan	*Enforcement Order* 39-12, *Enforcement Regulation* 22-10. *Administrative Guideline* issued on 1 June 2001 and partly revised on 20 June 2002 on intra-group services
United Kingdom	*Inland Revenue Tax Bulletin* Issues 31 (European Arbitration Convention), 37 (Transfer Pricing for Financial Transactions), 38 (Penalties), 43 (Advance Pricing Agreements), 46 (Non-Resident Landlords), 60 (Conduct Transfer Pricing Inquiries) and *Special Edition* April 2000 on 2003 UK/US Treaty (Mutual Agreement Procedure)
United States	Reg. § 1.482, Reg. § 1.6662-6

Table 4.3 Acceptable methods

Method	CUP	RP	CPL	PS	CP	TNM
OECD	Yes	Yes	Yes	Yes	No	Yes
China	Yes	Yes	Yes	Yes	Yes	Yes
Canada	Yes	Yes	Yes	Yes	No	Yes
France	Yes	Yes	Yes	Yes	No	Yes
Germany	Yes	Yes	Yes	Yes	No	Yes
Italy	Yes	Yes	Yes	Yes	Yes	No
Japan	Yes	Yes	Yes	Yes	No	Yes
United Kingdom	Yes	Yes	Yes	Yes	No	Yes
United States	Yes	Yes	Yes	Yes	Yes	No

Table 4.4 Priorities of methods

OECD	Transaction-based preferred over profit-based
China	Most appropriate method
Canada	Transaction-based preferred over profit-based
France	No priority
Germany	Transaction-based preferred over profit-based
Italy	Transaction-based preferred over profit-based
Japan	Transaction-based preferred over profit-based
United Kingdom	Transaction-based preferred over profit-based
United States	Best method

Table 4.5 Transfer pricing penalties

OECD	Ordinary penalties apply
China	Specific transfer pricing penalties apply
Canada	Specific transfer pricing penalties apply
France	Specific transfer pricing penalties apply
Germany	Specific transfer pricing penalties apply
Italy	Ordinary penalties apply
Japan	Ordinary penalties apply
United Kingdom	Ordinary penalties apply
United States	Specific transfer pricing penalties apply

Table 4.6 Reductions in penalties

OECD	No provision
China	No provision
Canada	Yes, under conditions
France	No provision
Germany	Yes, under conditions
Italy	Yes, under conditions
Japan	No provision
United Kingdom	Yes, under conditions
United States	Yes, under conditions

Table 4.7 Documentation requirements

OECD	Pricing decisions should be documented in accordance with prudent business practices. Reasonable for tax authorities to expect taxpayers to prepare and maintain such material. No contemporaneous obligation
China	Documents requested on a transfer pricing audit must be provided within 60 days of a request
Canada	Contemporaneous documentation required
France	Advance documentation effectively required
Germany	The economic and legal basis for arm's length prices and conditions in cross-border transactions with related parties must be documented
Italy	No statutory requirement but documentation recommended to avoid shifting burden of proof of reasonable prices to taxpayer. No contemporaneous documentation obligation
Japan	No statutory requirement but strongly recommended for audit defence. No contemporaneous documentation obligation
United Kingdom	Taxpayer should keep records and complete return
United States	Contemporaneous documentation required for penalty protection

Table 4.8 Return disclosures/related party disclosures

OECD	Should be limited to information sufficient to allow tax administration to determine which taxpayers need further examination
China	Form A-13 (for single type transactions) or Form B-13 (for multi-type transactions) of the annual income tax return
Canada	Form T106 requires disclosure of types of transactions, dollar amounts, related companies, and countries involved. methods used, and whether documentation requirements have been met
France	No specific disclosure required
Germany	No specific disclosure required
Italy	Tax Return (Form 'UNICO' – RF Section) requires disclosure of direct/indirect controlled by/of non-resident entities and relationships with non-resident entities under common control
Japan	Schedule 17 (3): Detailed Statement Concerning Foreign Affiliated Persons and Applied Transfer Pricing Methods
United Kingdom	No return disclosures except those required in statutory accounts. Annual reports are to be filed in compliance with any current Advance Pricing Agreements
United States	Forms 5471 and 5472

Table 4.9 Advance pricing agreements available

OECD	Unilateral and bilateral available
China	Unilateral and bilateral available
Canada	Unilateral and bilateral available. But bilateral preferred
France	Unilateral unavailable formally, but an informal process is developing
Germany	Available, but no formal procedure
Italy	Unilateral available
Japan	Unilateral and bilateral available. But bilateral preferred
United Kingdom	Unilateral and bilateral available. But bilateral preferred
United States	Unilateral and bilateral available

5
Associated Enterprises

Introduction

Transfer pricing takes place between any two or more constituent parts of a company, at least one of which is based in a host country. By the adroit use of pricing the seemingly legitimate transactions which take place between them, the company can attempt to avoid its full fiscal liabilities. To frustrate such practices and preserve the due revenues under the prevailing laws of their country, a taxation authority in the country concerned must be alert to the need to identify the characteristics of a foreign company operating within its jurisdiction and to understand its *modus operandi*. This includes the need for a careful definition of the structure and ownership of multinational companies for the purpose of ascertaining relationships between their constituent parts that could give rise to opportunities for transfer pricing abuses. In addition they need to bear in mind the full range of assets that can be the subject of traffic between two constituent parts of the same company.

Organizational structure

For related party transactions between a parent company and its foreign subsidiaries, or between such subsidiaries themselves, an appropriate transfer pricing policy can be established to fit the organization's structure and industrial character. From an organizational perspective, the objectives of transfer pricing are designed to provide reasonable measures of a subsidiary's economic performance, to motivate subsidiary managers, to preserve divisional autonomy, and to promote goal congruence. The following analysis stresses the behavioural effects of the pricing policy for an organization's internal transfers of assets.

Single focus business. This type of firm focuses its business on a single product or a restricted range of products. In its simplest form, a single product business serves a niche market. An organizational structure for a single product, unitary-focused business is depicted in Figure 5.1.

The corporation depicted only controls one entity, the profit center, while the latter serves a single market. In this case, sale prices depend upon the open market. Hence, there should be few, if any, transfer pricing issues.

Divisionalized multi-product business. Over time, a business might be expanded by moving existing products into a new market or by introducing new products into the current market. These actions not only lead to the need for a more complex organizational form, but also require the implementation of different competitive strategies in these differing markets. An alternative to the increased administrative complexity presented by this new form for a company, which has diversified into a number of product/market segments within a single

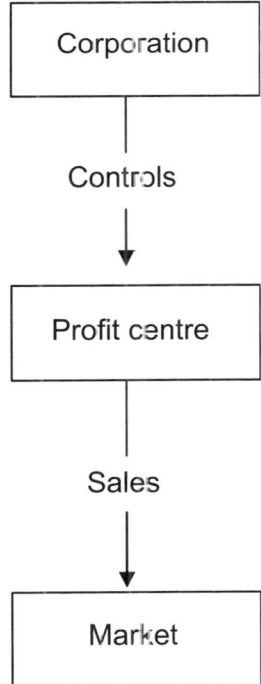

Figure 5.1 A single focus business model

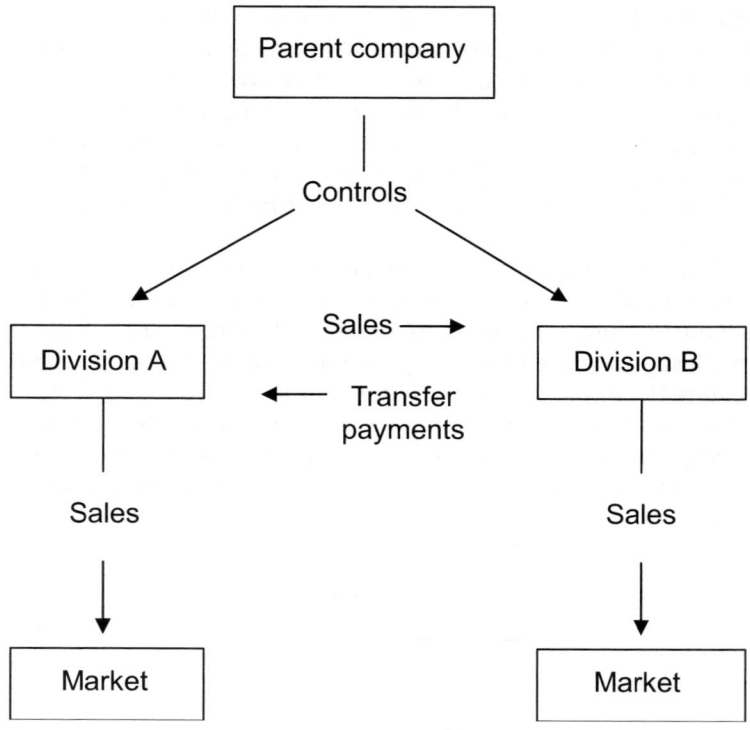

Figure 5.2 A divisionalized multi-product business model

business, is to subdivide the company into a number of divisions under the direction of divisional general managers. These managers are held responsible for both revenues and costs in their respective divisions, being often measured and rewarded on the basis of divisional profits. The need for an internal transfer pricing system arises when they exchange goods or services with each other. Figure 5.2 depicts a possible organizational structure of a divisionalized multi-product company.

In this model, Divisions A and B are controlled by a common company. The need for transfer pricing arises when the two Divisions exchange goods or services with each other. To illustrate this, when Division A sells a product or service to Division B, it will try to obtain the highest possible price from Division B to raise its own operating income. Correspondingly, Division B will try to obtain those goods at as low a price as possible. Consequently, managers of both Divisions have to take considerable interest in the prices they charge or pay because these inter-unit prices play a major part in the ability of the two Divisions to show a profit or a loss, bearing in mind that divisional managers are frequently evaluated on the basis of their unit's operating income.

Vertically integrated business. This is a common industrial structure for multinational enterprises. The vertical integration form enables a multinational enterprise to achieve economies of scale and scope in transaction costs, logistics, brand development, risk management, and technological and other intangible assets.

For reasons of size, most of a vertically integrated company is broken down into a variety of geographic and functional divisional units located in different countries. The divisions often trade with each other within the integrated group, each division being given responsibility for a specified set of activities in recognition of its superior information and skills regarding the use of resources and labour effectiveness that give it a measure of autonomy – operating independence from the group's central management. To measure financial performances effectively at the divisional level, some groups determine at their headquarters the transfer prices for the goods and services exchanged between any two or more of their divisions. Some groups expect their divisions to negotiate between themselves.

The model in Figure 5.3 illustrates multinational inter-group trades in a vertically integrated business and two sets of transfer prices established including:

1. The transfer of intermediate products from the semi-manufacturing division in country A to the finished goods manufacturing division in country B
2. The transfer of finished products from the finished goods manufacturing division in country B to the affiliated distributor in country C.

For intercompany trade between the divisions, internal transfer prices are used by the upstream division to attach a price to products transferred to the downstream division, located in a different country. Because divisional managers are held responsible for both revenues and costs in their own profit centres, and are often evaluated and rewarded on the basis of divisional profits, they take considerable interest in the price they pay or receive because this intercompany pricing plays a major part in showing a profit or a loss for their divisions.

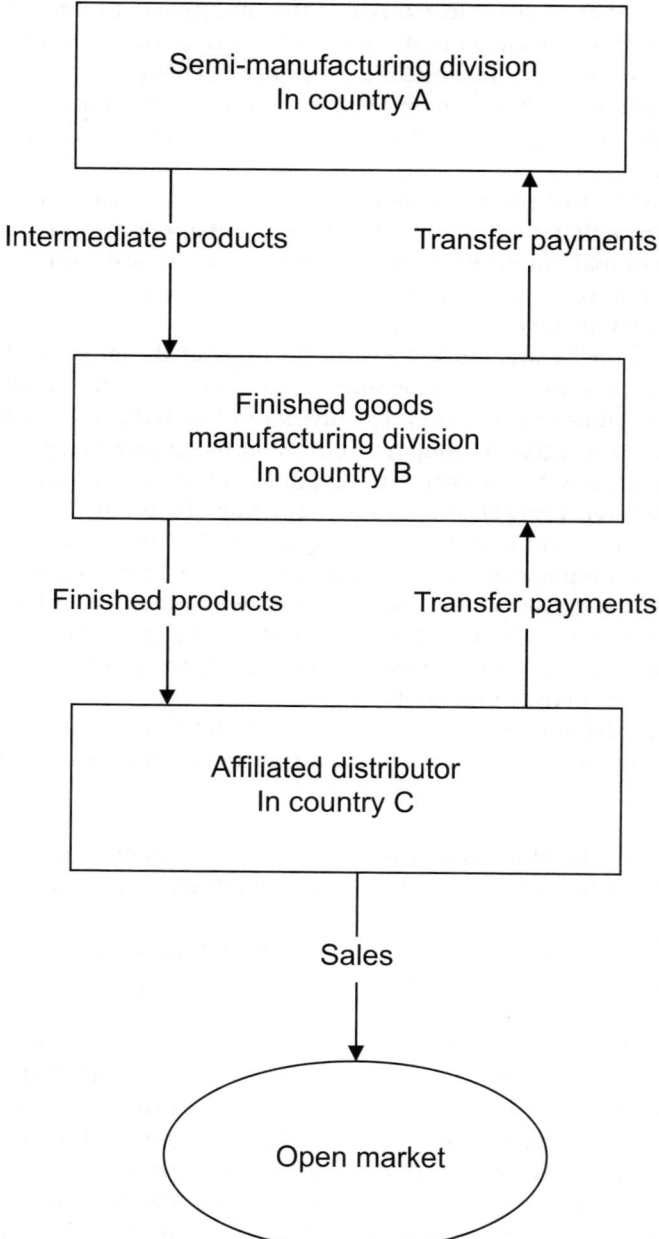

Figure 5.3 A vertically integrated business model

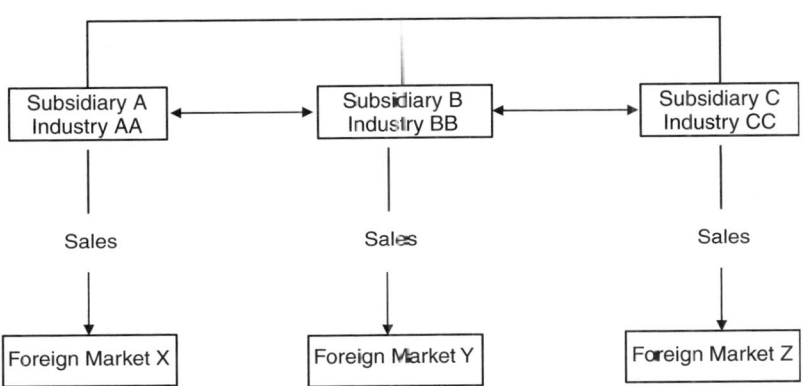

Figure 5.4 A conglomerate multinational enterprise model

Conglomerate. Another relatively complex structure of a multinational company can be the conglomerate, which uses its geographic spread of operations to achieve firm specific and location specific advantages. In addition to obtaining certain support services provided by headquarters in an attempt to minimize costs, overseas subsidiaries often require the expertise of the parent company in a conglomerate structure for the management of their own affairs and the determination of their business strategies. The parent company tends to allocate the joint costs of such functions incurred at headquarters among the various subsidiaries of the multinational system through transfer pricing. Figure 5.4 depicts the organizational structure of a conglomerate company, in which an interchange of assets and charges may take place between the various subsidiaries.

Related party identity

As with transfer pricing rules in other tax jurisdictions, the Chinese transfer pricing rules only apply to transactions that are conducted between or among related parties or controlled parties. An associated enterprise is defined in Article 52 of the *Detailed Implementing Rules of the Tax Law* as one whose business is based on the direct or indirect ownership or control of another party in respect of its capital, business operations, purchases or sales, or the direct or indirect ownership, or control by a third party common to both of them, or any other association which produces mutual benefits. A foreign enterprise and another company, enterprise or organization will be considered associated based on the tests of ownership and control, if one or more of the following circumstances prevails.

Ownership test

- Where a foreign enterprise directly or indirectly owns 25% or more of the total share capital of the Chinese company
- Where two enterprises are directly or indirectly owned by a third enterprise holding 25% or more share capital
- Where an enterprise borrows more than 50% of its loans from another enterprise, or where an enterprise guarantees 10% or more of the loans of another enterprise

Control

- Where one of the managing directors is, or half or more of the board of directors or the executive managers of an enterprise are, appointed by another enterprise
- Where an enterprise's production can only be operated with the provision of proprietary technology owned by another enterprise
- Where the provision of raw materials, parts, and semi-finished goods used by an enterprise in production are supplied or controlled by another enterprise
- Where the sales of the commodities of an enterprise are controlled by another enterprise
- Where the production, trading activities, and profits of an enterprise are effectively controlled by another enterprise having mutual benefits, such as the existence of family relationships.

Table 5.1 summarizes the relationship tests applying in the transfer pricing regulations of OECD, China, and other main industrial countries. It is worth noting that under China's transfer pricing rules, the relationship test of associated parties is very inclusive. A foreign investment enterprise or foreign enterprise can be deemed related to another entity for a variety of reasons, even where there is no actual legal ownership. For instance, in the case of a company whose purchases of raw materials or sales of products are controlled by another enterprise, their transactions come under the definition of related party transactions.

In practice, it is likely that some transactions may formally lie outside the concept of an 'associated enterprise' situation yet amount to the same thing. As an example, Figure 5.5 illustrates the nature of two possible indirectly related party transactions:

1. A Chinese subsidiary sells intermediate products to an overseas non-associated manufacturer. The sales prices are set up by its overseas parent firm.
2. The manufacturer re-processes the intermediate products and sells the final products to the non-associated parent company. The

Table 5.1 Relationship tests as defined in the transfer pricing regulations of China and other main industrial countries

Country	Relationship test	Shareholding
OECD	Associated enterprises	Not specified
China	Associated enterprises	25% or more
Canada	Not dealing at arm's length	Not specified
France	Common control	Not specified
Germany	Related persons	25% or more
Japan	Affiliated persons	50% or more
United Kingdom	Common control	Not specified
United States	Common control	Not specified

Source: Harrison and Glyn-Jones, 1999, p. 11

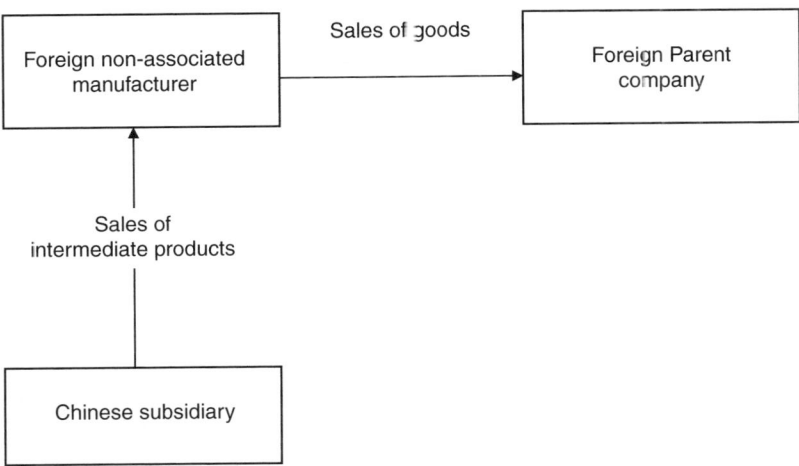

Figure 5.5 Indirectly related party transactions

manufacturer charges the parent company a price based on the purchasing and manufacturing costs.

To shift profits from the Chinese subsidiary to the overseas parent firm, the parent firm may have incentives to instruct the Chinese subsidiary to charge the non-associated manufacturing company a low price for the intermediate products. The manufacturing company in turn agrees to sell the finished product to the parent firm at a low price. Formally and legally in this case, the transactions between the Chinese subsidiary and the finished goods manufacturer are indirectly associated transactions, but the Chinese tax officials may still be concerned over the non-arm's length nature of transactions of this kind.

Related party transactions

Intercompany transactions include the transfer of tangible assets, intangible assets, the provision of services, and finance. The transfer pricing regulations detail these four major categories of reportable transactions with associated enterprises respectively as:

- The sale, use, and transfer of tangible property including buildings, vehicles, machinery, tools, and products
- The use and transfer of intangible property including land rights, copyrights, trade marks, brand names, patents, franchises, and designs
- The supply of services including those for market surveys, distribution, management, administration, production techniques, maintenance, design, consultation, agency functions, scientific research, and legal and accounting work
- The provision of funds including all kinds of long-term and short-term loans, guarantees, securities, interest-bearing advances, and deferred payments.

As illustrated in Figures 5.6 to 5.10, a Chinese subsidiary manufactures and sells its products to its foreign parent firm. The parent company provides assistance to the Chinese firm in the form of research and development, administrative services, and financing. The intercompany transactions involved for the transfer of tangible assets, intangible assets, the provision of services, and finance, have significant tax implications for both the subsidiary and its parent company.

Tangible assets. The term tangible assets refers to all the physical materials of a business. Foreign investment enterprises often rely on associated enterprises outside China for their raw materials, machines and equipment, and the sale of their finished products to other overseas affiliates or for direct marketing. The transactions involved for such arrangements often trigger transfer pricing investigations when purchases are overpriced and sales are underpriced, or when leasing fees for equipment are excessive. In Figure 5.6, the Chinese subsidiary manufactures a product which it sells to its parent firm abroad. The subsidiary may charge the parent company with product costs plus a certain profit percentage. Most foreign investment enterprises in China are process-exporting companies which import raw materials, machines, equipment, and intermediate products from overseas companies, and in turn sell their finished products abroad. In this case, purchases and sales are at the direction and under the control of the overseas parent company. Operations such as these provide substantial tax planning opportunities for multinational companies.

Intangible Assets. Transfer pricing for the sale and purchase of intangible property may typically involve patents and technical knowledge owned by an overseas parent company which licenses or sells such assets to a subsidiary or other foreign investment enterprise in China for its production or operational purposes. The OECD (1979) report recognizes that the prices set up by transnational corporations in relation to the transfer of technology 'present a number of difficulties for national tax authorities since the terms and conditions of such transfers may not correspond to the economic realities but may be used – partly because of the differences of national tax systems – as a means of shifting profit between members in order to alleviate the overall tax burden of the transnational corporation.' If the royalties and other payments for the transfer of intellectual property rights

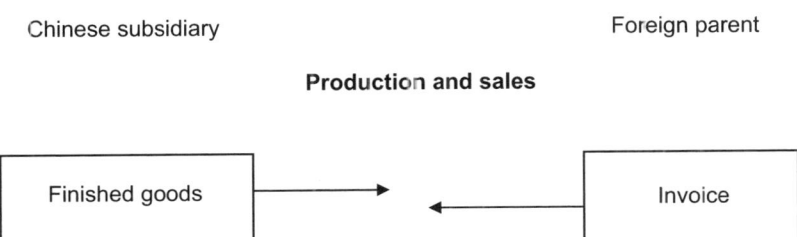

Figure 5.6   Intercompany transaction of tangible assets

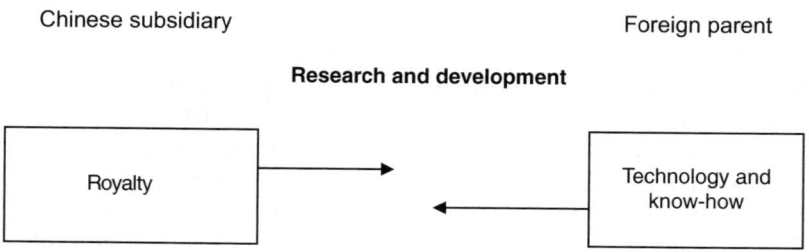

Figure 5.7 Intercompany transaction of intangible assets

charged by the parent firm are not of an arm's length nature, the tax authorities may adjust the amount of royalties claimed by the company in China for tax purposes. Royalties paid to overseas companies are deductible. In Figure 5.7, when the foreign parent firm provides technology and know-how, the subsidiary pays the parent in the form of royalties. To reduce taxable income, the company may pay excess royalty fees to its overseas parent company.

In the transfer pricing world, intangible property is often a major issue and of great concern for some companies in industries such as pharmaceuticals, automotive manufacturing, oil, and high-technology manufacturing. For example, the profitability of a pharmaceutical firm is highly reliant on expensive research and development to remain competitive in the open market. High research and development costs contribute to high drug costs. To protect its technical know-how, the company may engage in horizontal integration for internal transfers. In Figure 5.8, a multinational pharmaceutical group has three divisions – research division, production division, and sales division – respectively located in countries A, B and C. Transfer pricing occurs when tangible and intangible property are transferred from the research division to the production division, and finally, to the sales division.

A problem arises over how to establish a proper market price for setting the royalty fees which the research division will charge the

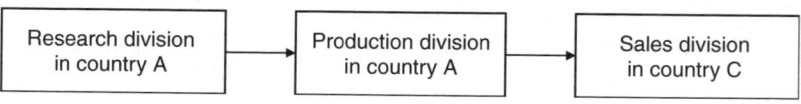

Figure 5.8 Transfer pricing in a pharmaceutical group

production division, reflecting research and development costs, and intellectual property rights. To generate both a lucrative market share and a premium price, the production and sales divisions respectively not only produce and sell the drugs but also perform additional activities that contribute extra value to the drugs, adding an intangible asset to the tangible assets of the company. An issue for taxation thereby may be created when the pharmaceutical firm determines the ownership of the added intangible assets and subsequently allocates licenses for production elsewhere.

Service assets. The staff members of a multinational's headquarters can provide a range of management services, including accounting, legal, and taxation advice, technical assistance associated with transfers of intangible assets, marketing know-how, and production knowledge. When a foreign investment enterprise provides such services to its associated enterprises free of charge or at unreasonably low rates, or when a foreign investment enterprise pays excessive fees for services provided by an associated enterprise, the Chinese tax authorities are likely to use fees for similar services paid by independent parties as the basis for an arm's length price. In Figure 5.9, the foreign parent firm provides management services and charges service fees to the Chinese subsidiary. The transfer of such services provides an opportunity for foreign investment companies to move profits out of China to avoid or reduce their income tax liabilities. To constrain such multinational tax avoidance manoeuvres, however, the Chinese tax law has stipulated that management fees paid to overseas parent firms cannot be deductible for taxation purpose, unless they apply to genuine charges for the provision of specific services required for specific business operations.

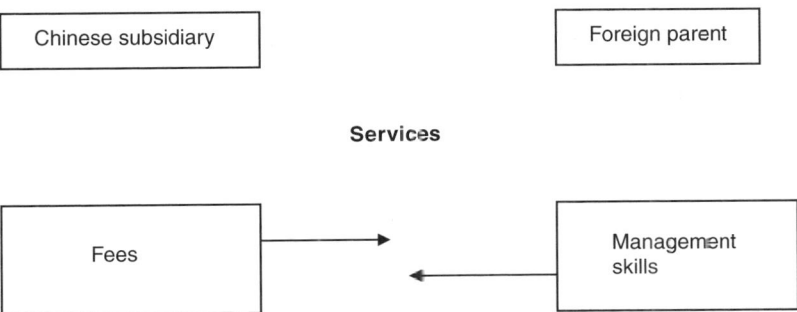

Figure 5.9 Intercompany transaction of services

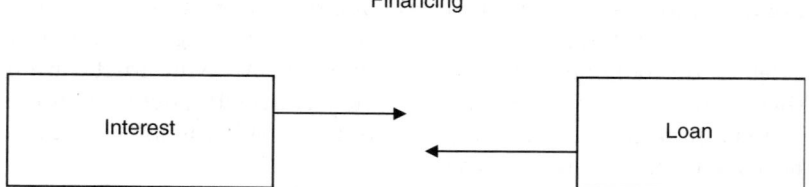

Figure 5.10 Intercompany transaction of financing

Financial assets. Financing through debt or equity has different tax effects. Transfer pricing usually comes into the reckoning when the interest rate used by a foreign investment enterprise in such transactions is higher or lower than the normal interest rate prevailing for similar transactions in the open market. If a foreign investment enterprise borrows funds from a related party and is charged an excessive interest rate on the loan, a transfer pricing investigation would be triggered.

In Figure 5.10, the foreign parent firm furnishes loans to the Chinese subsidiary and charges interest. In the light of the Chinese tax law, dividends paid to overseas investment companies cannot be deductible. From a tax planning strategy point of view, foreign investors may prefer to fund their Chinese subsidiaries by making significant loans rather than taking an equity interest. This is known as 'thin capitalization'. Taking advantage of this, the overseas parent company may then charge an excessive interest rate on the loan to move the Chinese company's profits out of China. The State Administration of Taxation has been keenly aware of the issue of thin capitalization. The Chinese rules stipulate that the range of the gearing ratio – debt to equity – should be 1:1 to 2.3:1.

Summary

Transfer pricing offers opportunities to minimize taxation. Companies based in foreign countries with associated companies in China can use their intercompany transactions for this purpose. The range of opportunities open to them is indicated in this chapter. The main variables governing these opportunities are the constitution and structure of the company, and the kinds of assets which can be made subject to such transfers.

6
Audit Adjustment Methods

Introduction

Globalization encourages and facilitates the growth of multinational internal markets. The World Trade Organization estimates that intercompany transactions among multinationals now account for about one-third of total world trade. This significant volume of intercompany transactions has important tax implications for both the multinational enterprises themselves and the agencies of governments that are charged with taxation management in the countries where they operate.

On the one hand are the multinational firms with strong incentives to shift profits made in countries with high tax jurisdictions to those with low tax jurisdictions. On the other hand are the revenue authorities of the countries which suffer the loss of revenues by such practices and which endeavour to prevent the future tax avoidance activities of multinational enterprises. Consequently, more and more revenue authorities are now focusing their legislative, regulative, and enforcement efforts on multinational transfer pricing practices. They have unanimously adopted the arm's length standard as the most principled approach to deal with the transfer pricing issue. China is not an exception.

Arm's length principle

The arm's length principle uses the pricing behaviour of an independent firm in an uncontrolled transaction as the benchmark for determining transfer prices in similar transactions between members of a multinational group, or company units which have an *a priori* special relationship. In applying the arm's length principle to a multinational enterprise to determine the price levels of its transfer pricing, a national tax authority attempts to neutralize the effect of any ownership or other associational relationship between members on the transfer prices they adopt when they deal with each other.

The arm's length principle is stated in Paragraph 1 of Article 9 of the OECD *Model Tax Convention*. The need for it is manifest (when) 'conditions are made or imposed between ...two associated enterprises in their commercial or financial relations which differ from those which would be made between independent enterprises, (so that) any profits which would, but for those conditions, have accrued to one of the enterprises, but, by reason of those conditions, have not so accrued, may be included in the profits of that enterprise and taxed accordingly.'

Like most other countries, the Chinese transfer pricing legislation is based on the arm's length principle. Article 13 of the *Income Tax Law of the People's Republic of China for Enterprises with Foreign Investment and Foreign Enterprises (Tax Law)* stipulates that the prices charged or paid in business dealings between the establishments of foreign investment enterprises within China and their associated enterprises should be the same as the prices charged or paid in comparable uncontrolled transactions between independent, unrelated enterprises. Under Article 13 of the *Tax Law*, if the transactions are not carried out at arm's length and, thus, result in a reduction of taxable income, the tax authorities have the right to make reasonable adjustments.

The arm's length principle requires that the consideration charged in cross-border associated party transactions is comparable to the consideration charged by independent parties. The comparisons may be based on either 'external comparable prices' using prices charged in the

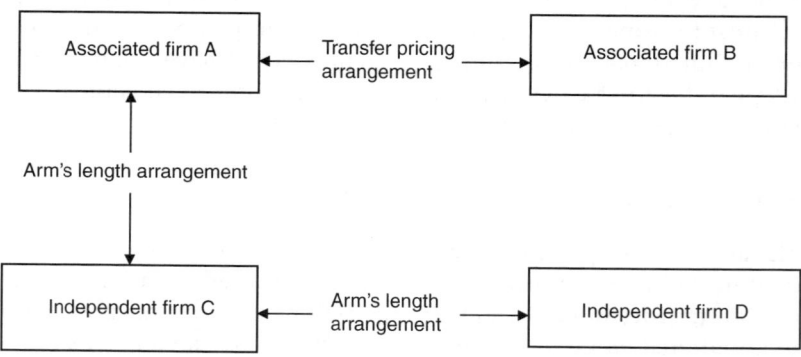

Figure 6.1 The arm's length principle

open market for comparable transactions, or 'internal generated comparable prices' using prices paid or charged by the taxpayer in transactions with unrelated parties. An example, as illustrated in Figure 6.1, supposes that company A sells goods to its associated firm B. In seeking price comparisons for the product flow between the two associated companies, company A may investigate sales of similar products between completely independent companies C and D. In case the data for such transactions are unavailable in the open market, company A may use its own sales to an unrelated company C as the benchmark.

Transfer pricing methods

According to the Chinese transfer pricing rules, the prices charged to tangible assets should have a clear transaction base. Owing to the lack of reliable public data in China, however, the tax authorities are willing to consider that other reasonable methods, such as profit-based methods, are appropriate for calculating the prices of transactions.

Transaction-based methods compare the prices in transactions between related companies with similar transactions between unrelated companies. Transaction-based methods include comparable uncontrolled price, resale price, and cost plus. Profit methods compare the profit margins for deals between related companies with similar transactions between unrelated companies. In situations where relevant pricing data are not available, the profit methods are more appropriate, profit data being more readily obtained. Under the transfer pricing rules, three profit-based methods – the profit split, comparable profit, and transactional net margin – are highlighted as other reasonable methods, but so far no detailed guidelines on the profit methods have been provided in China.

As for transactions involving intercompany provisions of services, loans, and the transfer of other assets, no particular methods are laid down for determining arm's length results. Arm's length prices under such circumstances are broadly referred to as any payments or receipts that a third party would agree to for the same kind of transaction.

Comparable uncontrolled price method. Under the Chinese transfer pricing regulations, comparable uncontrolled price compares prices paid or charged by a foreign direct enterprise to related parties with those of comparable transactions of the foreign direct enterprise with unrelated parties. The taxable income is determined in accordance with the price in identical or similar transactions between unrelated entities. The comparable uncontrolled price requires a high degree of comparability between the assets being transferred in the two transactions. In seeking comparable data, a company may need to investigate sales of similar products completed between unrelated entities. In case the data for unrelated party transactions are unavailable in the public domain, the company may use data of its own sales or purchases to an unrelated party for the purpose.

The use of the comparable uncontrolled price method, however, can make it extremely difficult to take account of the full range of variables and material differences that occur between intercompany as opposed to third party transactions. The main data that serve as a basis for assessing the comparability of the assets transferred, and which thereby provide the means to justify imposed tax adjustments, include the following.

- Transaction facts such as the date and place of transactions, delivery terms and procedures, the volumes involved, and warranty arrangements
- Transaction client details, such as whether the transactions are conducted with manufacturers, distributors, retailers, or exporters
- Product characteristics and details, such as type of product, brand name, specifications, performance or function, shape, structure, and packaging
- Information about the environment – social, political, and economic – of a product's market destination.

Comparable uncontrolled price method model. As illustrated in Figure 6.2, a Chinese subsidiary purchases assets such as products from its parent firm in a foreign country. If the prices paid are regarded by the tax authority as other than arm's length in nature, to determine and adjust these purchase prices, the Chinese tax inspectors may refer to the company's purchases of similar products from an unrelated firm A in the same foreign country, or to purchases and sales between two completely unrelated firms A and B.

Resale price method. Under the Chinese transfer pricing regulations, the resale price method focuses on the price at which goods purchased from a related party are resold to an unrelated party, less an allowance for a gross profit margin. The taxable income is determined in accordance with the reasonable resale profit margin to be gained from the price at which the goods are resold by the affiliated enterprise to independent entities. There is less concern with the comparability of products than in the comparable uncontrolled pricing method. The

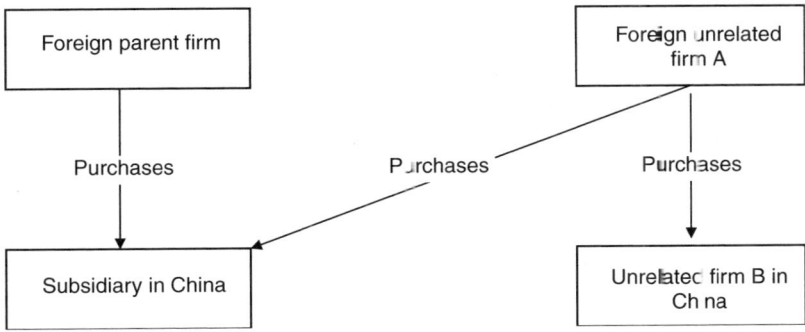

Figure 6.2 Comparable uncontrolled price method model

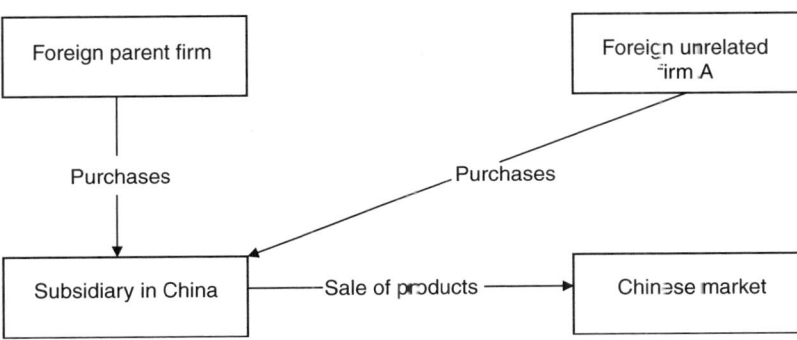

Figure 6.3 Resale price method model

resale price method is limited to cases where the reseller has only undertaken simple processing or a purely purchase and resale function with little value added to the product other than those accruing from normal sales, marketing, and distribution activities. Hence, any significant change of the shape, performance, structure, or brand name of the assets would disqualify this method. The determination of the gross profit margin should take into account the functions performed, assets used, and risks assumed by the reseller. The resale price method is probably most useful when applied to marketing operations.

Resale price method model. As illustrated in Figure 6.3, a Chinese subsidiary purchases assets such as finished products from its parent firm and an unrelated firm A in the same foreign country. All products purchased are distributed to third party customers in the Chinese market. It is assumed that the Chinese company performs the same functions with respect to the products from both sources. As such, the gross margins earned on the purchases from the unrelated firm A could be used to determine the arm's length price of the products purchased from the foreign parent firm. If the functions performed, assets used, and risks assumed respectively in the related party and the unrelated party transactions differ, an assessment must be made as to whether such differences materially affect the gross margins earned in the two transactions. Where the differences do affect the gross margins earned and the effect of the differences cannot be reliably estimated, it will not be possible to apply the resale price method using the uncontrolled transaction to determine an arm's length price.

Cost plus method. The cost plus method involves taking account of the costs of manufacturing the product plus a normal profit margin that would accrue from the sales of similar products elsewhere. The taxable income is determined by reference to the mark-up achieved by a comparable seller in similar transactions with independent entities, plus reasonable costs and fees. The cost plus method is generally simple to administer and understand. Furthermore, the data needed for using it are usually readily available. The disadvantage of it as a method is that the incentives for manufacturing companies to reduce their costs are weakened, and that, accordingly, the profit margin for the final selling firm becomes constricted.

Cost plus method model. As illustrated in Figure 6.4, a Chinese subsidiary purchases raw materials from unrelated suppliers. After processing the raw materials, it then sells its manufactures to its parent firm and an unrelated firm A in the same foreign country. It is assumed that the Chinese company performs the same functions with respect to the products sold to both its parent firm and the unrelated firm A. As such,

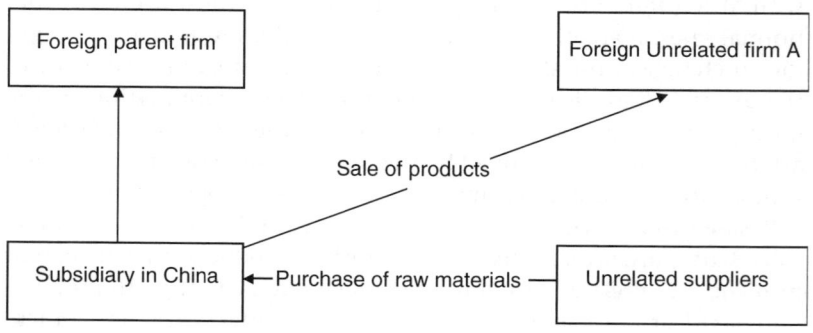

Figure 6.4 Cost plus method model

the gross margins earned on the sales to the unrelated firm A could be used to determine the arm's length price of the products sold to the parent firm. If the functions performed, assets used, and the risks assumed in the related party and unrelated party transactions differ, an assessment must be made as to whether those differences materially affect the gross margins earned in the two transactions. Where any such differences do affect the gross margins earned and their effect cannot be reliably estimated, it will not be possible to apply the cost plus method using the uncontrolled transaction to determine an arm's length price.

Profit split method. The profit split method is based upon the economic notion of joint venture or partnership relationship. It divides profits generated by a transaction between associated companies according to the relative economic value of each firm's contribution to that transaction. The profit split method depends on profit comparisons rather than price or transaction comparisons and functional analyses. The profit split method calculates an arm's length net profit for each of the related parties by identifying the overall profit to be split between the related parties, and splitting it according to the relative contributions made by each party to the creation of that profit.

There are two approaches to profit split.

- Contribution analysis approach. Contribution analysis divides the combined profit arising from the controlled transaction between the associated parties on the basis of the relative economic value of the functions performed, risks assumed, and resources employed by each party.
- Residual analysis approach. Residual analysis consists of a two-step process. First, each participant is allocated a basic return appropriate for the type of transaction in which it is engaged. The second step consists of allocating the residual profit among the associated parties according to the unique or highly valuable assets contributed by each party.

Profit split method model. As illustrated in Figure 6.5, the foreign parent company provides raw materials, equipment, spare parts, services, and key production techniques to the Chinese subsidiary. The Chinese company assembles the finished products and sells them to its foreign related firm A. Company A markets and distributes the products in the foreign market, both companies being in the same country as the parent company.

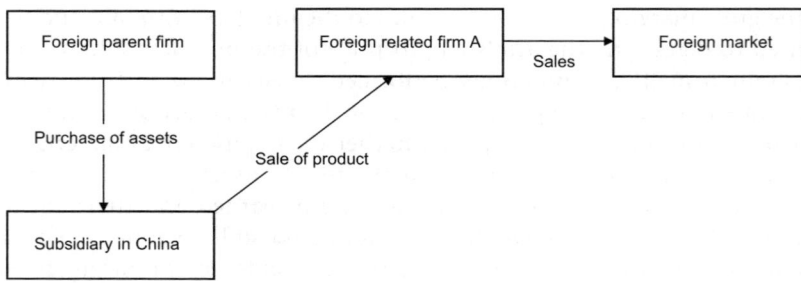

Figure 6.5 Profit split method model

Table 6.1 Functional analysis for a profit split method audit for the case in Figure 6.5

Functions	Risks	Intangible Goods
Foreign Parent Firm Product research, design and development Technical service	**Foreign Parent Firm** Foreign exchange volatility	**Foreign Parent Firm** Patent and technical know–how Trade mark and brand names
Subsidiary in China Production of finished goods and quality control Packaging and labelling of products. Shipping of products	**Subsidiary in China** Defective products and warranties Product obsolescence	**Subsidiary in China** Technical data
Foreign Related Firm A Marketing Shipping products to customers	**Foreign Related Firm B** Arranging product liability insurance Inventory and marketing Credit and foreign exchange	**Foreign Related Firm A** Customer list After-sales services Sales force

The functional analysis of the three entities is summarized in Table 6.1. Since no comparable data are available, the application of the comparable uncontrolled price, resale price, and cost plus methods for audit purposes are precluded. The profit split may then be utilized to determine transfer prices. The contributions of assets, risks, and functions to the production and selling of the product are assessed as 40% for the parent company, 35% for the Chinese subsidiary, and 25%

for company A. If the combined operating profit from the total sales is RMB 200,000, the profit split at the net profit level is RMB 80,000 for the parent, RMB 70,000 for the Chinese subsidiary, and RMB 50,000 for company A.

Comparable profit method. The comparable profit method determines an arm's length profit by comparing a company's net profit margin generated by its controlled transactions, with the return obtained by a firm engaged in comparable uncontrolled transactions. Net profit margins are measured by the use of appropriate profit level indicators such as the return on assets, or operating income in relation to sales. In the application of the comparable profits method, a functional analysis of the associated enterprise on one side, and that of the independent enterprise on the other, is required to determine whether the transactions are comparable and what adjustments should be made to obtain reliable results. The comparable profit method depends on profit comparisons rather than on price or transaction comparisons.

Comparable profit method model. As illustrated in Figure 6.6, a Chinese subsidiary sells 30% of the total sales of its products to its foreign parent firm and a further 40% to an unrelated firm A which acts as the master distributor of the products in the same foreign country. Meanwhile, it also sells the balance of 30% of the total sales of its products to an unrelated firm B as a retailer in China's domestic market. The comparable profit method is selected to test the arm's length nature of the transfer prices between the Chinese subsidiary and its parent firm. Two comparable unassociated companies A and B have been identified as being functionally similar. The net margin information is available, making it suitable to apply this method for an audit.

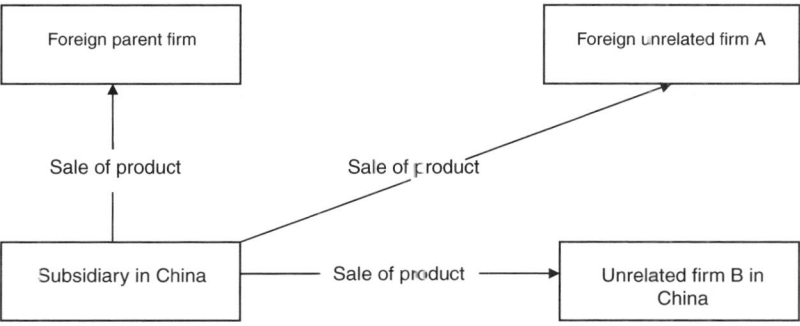

Figure 6.6 Comparable profit method model

Transactional net margin method. The Chinese regulations describe the transactional net margin as a method to determine an arm's length profit by comparing the net profit margin obtained by an associated enterprise with that which is obtained by a comparable independent firm. The comparable profit method deals with income, whereas the transactional net profit margin method deals with pricing. The comparable profit method and the transactional net margin method may be used interchangeably in practice.

Selecting the transfer pricing method

According to the Chinese transfer pricing rules, the prices for tangible assets must be based on transaction-based methods such as comparable uncontrolled price, resale price, and cost plus. Comparable uncontrolled price is primarily concerned with the product being transferred, whereas resale price and cost plus focus on the functions being performed.

Theoretically, comparable uncontrolled price is the most preferred method and should be used whenever possible. Resale price is the second most preferred method. Cost plus is the least preferred method. In practice, the Chinese tax authorities tend to use cost plus to calculate/adjust the value of related party transactions. All three approaches should separately result in the determination of the same arm's length price.

The application of the transaction-based methods is subject to the availability of comparable data. In practice, vertically integrated multinational groups may achieve profits that substantially exceed the combined profits of non-integrated firms performing similar functions. This may preclude comparisons with independent firms. For example, an independent manufacturing firm typically has additional sales and marketing expenses, and risks which a vertically integrated manufacturer selling products to its affiliates as scheduled does not have. In the frequently found cases in which comparable data are unavailable or are difficult to obtain, the profit-based methods, such as profit split, comparable profit, and transactional net profit, would be the alternative approaches for use in determining the arm's length pricing of associated party transactions.

In selecting a transfer pricing method, a company's final choice of method should depend on the recognized need to be able to

- **Assess** the potential application of each transfer pricing method chosen to each identified transfer pricing transaction using the comparable data

Table 6.2 Characteristics of the transfer pricing methods used for audits

Transfer pricing method	Method base	Data for comparison	Level of analysis	Type of transaction	Comparable data identified
CUP	Transaction	Sales or purchases	Product	Tangibles Intangibles Services	Market prices of comparable transactions
RP	Transaction	Gross profit margin	Functions, assets, and risks	Tangibles Services	Gross margins of functionally comparable transactions
CPL	Transaction	Gross profit margin	Functions, assets, and risks	Finances	Gross margins of functionally comparable transactions
PS	Profit	Net profit margin	Functions, assets, and risks	Tangibles Intangibles Services	Limited comparable data available but global profit or transactions identified easily
CP	Profit	Net profit margin	Profit comparison	Tangibles Services	Comparable data available in respect of the net margins earned in functionally comparable transactions

Note: CUP = Comparable Uncontrolled Price, RP = Resale Price, CPL = Cost Plus, PS = Profit Split, CP = Comparable Profit

- **Justify** the reasons for selecting one transfer pricing method over another as the most appropriate method for a particular transfer pricing transaction
- **State** the reasons for rejecting certain transfer pricing methods as being inappropriate for a particular transfer pricing transaction.

Table 6.2 summarizes the features of the typically used transfer pricing methods.

Double taxation and competent authority

Multinational cross-border transactions by definition involve at least two countries with separate tax jurisdictions. Tax authorities in different countries may hold different views on what price should be attached to the same transaction. To ensure a fair share of a company's tax liability, each country uses its own particular approach to the adjustment of the profits of a company operating in its tax jurisdiction. The respective claims of the two or more countries concerned may result in an audit controversy, that is, transfer pricing adjustments by tax authorities under different transfer pricing rules could create tax conflicts between revenue authorities and, in the end, lead to double taxation, where a multinational group can receive a demand to pay tax on income which had already been taxed elsewhere.

A simplified consolidated profit and loss account for two companies in Table 6.3 illustrates how double taxation can occur. In this example, a foreign investment subsidiary company in China manufactures and sells a consignment of goods direct to its foreign parent company at a transfer price of US$ 30,000. With manufacturing costs of US$ 20,000, the subsidiary reports profits of US$ 10,000 to the Chinese tax authority for tax purposes. The parent company sells the goods to overseas markets at a price of US$ 50,000. Taking into account the costs of US$ 30,000 charged by the subsidiary, plus its own sales expenses of US$ 5,000, the parent company declares profits

Table 6.3 Profit adjustment and double taxation (US$)

Elements of the case	Chinese subsidiary	Foreign parent company	Consolidated
Sales to the overseas market by parent company	0	50,000	50,000
Sales to parent company	30,000	0	0
Manufacturing costs	20,000	0	20,000
Sales expenses	0	5,000	5,000
Cost of goods from subsidiary	0	30,000	0
Total profits as declared to taxation authorities	10,000	15,000	25,000
Chinese tax authority's claim to taxable income	12,000	0	
Foreign tax authority's claim to taxable income	0	15,000	

of US$ 15,000 to the overseas tax authority. For the entire set of transactions, the total taxable income of the multinational company as a whole is US$ 25,000.

However, the Chinese tax authority may decide that the transfer prices charged to the parent should be adjusted to US$ 12,000, representing additional earned income in China. The multinational group would then be liable for tax on a total income of US$ 27,000. Because this change of the transfer price will have no effect on the consolidated profits of the company as a whole, the multinational's total income remains at US$ 25,000. As such, US$ 2,000 of this income may be taxed twice. In an attempt to relieve this double taxation, the multinational can apply to its own tax authority suitably to reduce its tax liability as assessed, in view of the intervention by the Chinese tax authority and its imposition of the arm's length principle on the transaction in question. If the company's domestic tax authority accepts the validity of the Chinese adjustment, and that the requested relief is justifiable, acting as the competent authority in the case it may then directly consult the relevant Chinese tax authority to negotiate a resolution.

The State Administration of Taxation has been aware of the potential double taxation problem for multinationals when other tax jurisdictions do not approve a tax relief for adjustments already made in China. To address the issue, the State Administration of Taxation issued the *Provisional Measures for People's Republic of China Residents (Nationals) to Apply for Tax Mutual Consultation Process* (effective from 1 July 2005). These measures provide for a competent authority procedure operating for Chinese residents. In practice, the process is intragovernmental and is quite time-consuming. In addition, there may be difficulties in getting one country to accept adjustments initiated by another country.

Summary

The vast number of foreign companies operating in China do so on a variety of footings. Their relationships with parent companies or other associates outside of China are very varied, constituting a wide spectrum of forms. Consequently, although the arm's length principle is the standard requirement of China's tax authorities for the determination of prices for transactions between related parties, the kaleidoscopic conditions found in practice make it impossible to apply one simple means either for determining such prices by the companies themselves, or for the tax authorities to take corrective steps to adjust such prices when they have been found to be subject to malpractice.

A range of methods are available for use by both sides from which the most suitable one can be selected according to circumstances. China's government has specified its own order of preference in the use of these methods in urging foreign companies to conform to the requirement of the arm's length principle. China's policy is to collect justifiable taxes under the existing laws but not to expose a company to double taxation, a possibility which it recognizes, and for which it is prepared to make due allowances.

7
Documentation and Penalties

Introduction

In China, as in most other countries, the burden of proof that the arm's length price in related party transactions has been used rests with the taxpayer. In addition to the disclosure requirements of related party transactions in their financial statements, foreign investment enterprises and foreign enterprises are required to disclose information about their related party transactions on their annual corporate tax returns. In a transfer pricing audit, the Chinese tax authorities have the right to require that a company provides information to support its decisions over transfer pricing (Article 18 of SAT *Circular* No. 59, April 1998).

Current requirements

The information that would then be requested includes the following.

- Detailed information relating to transactions with related enterprises and third parties, such as sales and purchases, financing, provision of services, assignments of tangible and intangible assets, and grants of rights for the use of tangible and intangible assets
- Detailed information on elements that affect the prices for transactions, such as the volume, place, form of the product, trade marks, and terms of payment
- Other relevant information associated with determining the transactional prices or basis for charges. The early preparation of such documentation would greatly save compliance costs for taxpayers, as opposed to retrospective compilation.

Table 7.1 Advised quality levels of processes and documentation for dealings with foreign associated enterprises

Low quality	Medium quality	High quality
No analysis of functions, assets, risks, market conditions, and business strategies	Inadequate analysis of functions, assets, risks, market conditions, and business strategies	Sound analysis of functions, assets, risks, market conditions, and business strategies
No taxpayer documentation or processes to enable a check on selection of methodologies	Insufficient taxpayer documentation or processes to enable a check on selection of methodologies	Selection of method fully supported with contemporaneous documentation
No comparables used.	Comparability based on limited data from independent dealings	Comparability based on adequate data from independent dealings. Application of method fully supported with contemporaneous documentation
No effort to implement and review arm's length transfer pricing policies	Limited effort to implement and review arm's length transfer pricing policies	Genuine effort to implement and review arm's length transfer pricing policies

Contemporaneous transfer pricing documentation is that which is created at the same time that terms are set and the transactions carried out. At present, taxpayers are not specifically required to maintain contemporaneous documentation. But the State Administration of Taxation has drafted the ruling for contemporaneous documentation requirements. The draft is currently being circulated for consultation at the State Administration of Taxation level. The issuance of formal contemporaneous documentation requirements is expected in the near future. The new rules are likely to require a detailed list of principal documents and explanations to support the taxpayer's transfer pricing arrangements.

The Australian approach. To avoid the transfer pricing audit, it is crucial for the taxpayer to demonstrate to the tax authority that the transfer prices are in accord with the arm's length principle. With regard to the preparation of documentation, the Australian Tax Office

(ATO) has provided a useful methodology for developing the documentation to support transfer prices. In designing its transfer pricing policy, a company could refer to the Australian specifications.

The Australian approach consists of a four-step process, each step of it providing documentary evidence that the requirements have been properly met. The process involves the following steps.

1. A description of the transfer pricing transactions in the context of the taxpayer's business
2. The means and criteria used to select the most appropriate transfer pricing method
3. The application of the most appropriate transfer pricing method in practice
4. The determination and demonstration of the arm's length principle as an outcome.

In addition, the Australian Tax Office has issued guidance for taxpayers to gauge the quality of their documentation, as shown in Table 7.1.

For a detailed exposition of the process and documentation, reference can be made to the Australian Tax Office's Taxation Ruling, TR 98/11, *Income Tax: Documentation and Practical Issues Associated with Setting and Reviewing Transfer Pricing in International Dealings*.

Maintenance of documentation

In cases where a taxpayer's business is complex and the taxpayer conducts a large number of related party transactions, the transfer pricing documentation required of the taxpayer can be very detailed. As a result, the preparation of such documentation may be expensive and time-consuming. It is important for the taxpayer to retain such documentation for use in a future income year. The documentation may include a functional analysis of the parties, describing the functions performed, assets used, and risks assumed by the business in its transaction with related parties, and a justification for the transfer pricing methods actually chosen.

Tax auditors in China are bound by the secrecy requirements of Article 45 of *Tax Administration Rules and Procedures for Transactions between Related Parties* (State Administration of Taxation Circular No. 59) to ensure that no public disclosure of a company's transfer pricing policies, and or information derived from a company's business documents during audit, takes place.

Functional analysis

From an auditor's point of view, a functional analysis is necessary to understand the qualitative nature of the work, assets, and risks undertaken by a company, so that a comparison can be made with other enterprises that undertake similar work, and with similar assets and risks. The State Administration of Taxation acknowledges the importance of the functional analysis in the *Implementation Rules for Advance Pricing Arrangements for Transactions between Related Parties* (Guo Shui Fa [2004] No. 118). The rules state that in the application for an advance pricing agreement, a functional analysis is a necessary component of the documentation which the taxpayer is required to prepare to support his transfer pricing position. The functional analysis can also be used to assist the taxpayer to support the selection and application of a particular transfer pricing method.

Functions can be conceived as the activities performed by each of the associated companies engaged in a particular cross-border transaction as a normal part of its operations. The functional analysis assists in the identification of the factors that contribute to the profits earned from the transaction as a whole and the respective contributions to it made by each party involved.

A general functional analysis is the means enabling the auditor

- To identify the degree of complexity involved in each of the identified functions performed
- To identify the level of risk associated with the functions undertaken by the audited party – over such elements as inventory, technology, obsolescence, product quality, research and development, warranty, foreign exchange, and insurance
- To identify comparable entities.

A functional analysis should result in the identification of four general categories as follows.

- Manufacturing functions – such as materials purchasing, inventory, production equipment and scheduling, manufacturing and processing engineering, packaging and labeling, quality control, shipping of products
- Research and development – such as the generation of intangible goods, and the production and marketing of intangible goods

- Marketing functions – such as marketing and product strategies, advertising, and trade shows
- Administrative and selling functions such as pricing policy, accounting, legal, computer processing, finance, insurance, and personnel.

Meanwhile, in the functional analysis the possible risks assumed that should be taken into account include

- Market risk
- Inventory risk – including raw materials, work in process, and finished goods
- Defective products and warranty
- Credit and bad debt risk
- Foreign exchange risk
- Environmental risk.

In the functional analysis, the OECD Guidelines recommend a variety of comparability factors that need to be considered, including the following.

- Characteristics of property or services – such as their physical features, their quality and reliability, their availability and volume of supply, the nature and extent of services, the form of the transaction involved, and the type of intangible property – such as patents, trademarks, and know-how – involved
- Functions performed and risks assumed. The principal functions performed that should be identified include design, manufacturing, assembling, research and development, servicing, purchasing, distribution, marketing, advertising, transportation, financing, and management. The types of risks to consider include market risks such as input cost and output price fluctuations, risks of loss associated with the investment in and use of property, plant and equipment, the risks of success or failure of investment in research and development, and financial risks such as those caused by currency exchange rate fluctuations, interest rate variability, and credit risks
- Contractual terms – such as the currency used for payments, credit and payment terms, the duration of the contract, and the extent of guarantees or support
- Economic circumstances – such as the geographic location of the market, the size of the market, the extent of competition in the market, the relative competitive positions of the buyers and sellers,

the availability of substitute goods and services, the levels of supply and demand in the market as a whole and in particular regions, consumer purchasing power, the nature and extent of government regulation of the market, costs of production, and transport costs
- Business strategies – such as innovation and new product development, degree of diversification, risk aversion, assessment of political changes, input of existing and planned labour laws, and other factors bearing upon the daily conduct of business. Besides these, an important business strategy is to devise market penetration schemes. Multinational enterprises enter foreign markets by establishing subsidiaries or branches. To support an infant subsidiary abroad in its competition with local firms, the parent company might temporarily charge a price for its product or licensing that is lower than the price chargeable in the open market. Alternatively, the subsidiary might temporarily incur higher start-up costs or costs for increased marketing efforts, resulting in lower profit levels than for those of other companies operating in the same market. The key issue for a market penetration scheme is judging whether the costs of devising and implementing the scheme will be justified by future profits or an expansion of market share that will be obtained by it.

Cost sharing agreement

A cost sharing arrangement involves an agreement whereby two or more persons or entities agree to share the costs and risks of research and the development of new, intangible property, as they are incurred, in exchange for a specified interest in any such property that is successfully created. Cost sharing arrangements offer greater certainty with respect to transfer pricing and the defined ownership of the intellectual property developed.

Formal implementation rules on cost sharing arrangements have not yet been issued in China. However, in a private ruling letter issued in 2004, the State Administration of Taxation endorsed an international research and development cost sharing arrangement. The private ruling letter provides that under certain conditions, not only are the outbound research and development cost sharing payments tax deductible for the foreign investment enterprise making a remittance from China, but the payments will also not be subject to withholding tax. Therefore, while a royalty is subject to withholding tax, the cost sharing payment will be exempted – a very valuable condition for companies which cannot take advantage of the withholding tax credits (Ernst and Young, 2004a; Chong and De Souza, 2005).

Fines and charges

For the late filing of the related party transactions declaration, penalties can be imposed, ranging from RMB 2,000 to RMB 10,000. If the taxpayer fails to provide adequate information, a transfer pricing adjustment being made subsequent to an audit, however, can be punitive. A company must pay tax on the increased taxable income arising from a transfer pricing adjustment. In addition, if the enterprise does not adjust its accounting books to show the prices or fees that the auditors determined should have been paid to the related party – and therefore the excess which should be refunded by the related party – the amount of the adjustment will also be treated as a deemed dividend. This deemed dividend, if deemed paid to a foreign party, will be subject to a 20% withholding tax. The withholding tax rate may be reduced under a tax treaty, depending on the definition of dividends in the particular treaty concerned.

For any adjustments made on a royalty or interest that has been paid to the foreign party and that has already been subject to withholding tax, no refunds on any withholding tax previously paid will be granted (Article 10 of State Administration of Taxation circular [1992] No. 237, October 1992). For any tax payments resulting from a transfer pricing investigation, the taxpayer must settle the payment within the time limit prescribed by the tax authorities. If the taxpayer fails to pay the tax within the time limit, a surcharge of 0.05% per day and, for serious violations, up to five times that amount, may be imposed on the delinquent taxpayer.

Summary

A phenomenon in business practice in the economically developed countries of the world today is compliance costs. Governmental supervision of commercial activity has inevitably led to impositions of a documentary nature that can make time consuming and cost demands of expensive proportions. With the advent of closer attention by governments to the practices and abuses of transfer pricing, there has arrived an increasingly detailed body of documentary requirements that must accompany all cross-border transactions, imposed in an effort to ensure that the arm's length principle prevails and that a company's full tax liabilities are met.

China is no exception to this trend. In having perhaps a greater need to make such compliance impositions than most other countries, it has duly established a range of penalties for non-compliance.

8
Advance Pricing Agreements

Introduction

An advance pricing agreement is an arrangement between a taxpayer and the relevant tax authority setting out the methods that will be used for calculating the prices for intended related party transactions in advance of the event. Advance pricing agreements may cover a wide variety of transactions, namely the sale and use of tangible assets, the transfer and use of intangible assets, the provision of services, and financial transactions. Advance pricing agreements are avenues for taxpayers to negotiate acceptable business arrangements with the tax authorities. In advance pricing agreements, the tax authority agrees with the taxpayer's preferred transfer pricing method before the taxpayer conducts the intended transactions. Advance pricing agreements are widely available in OECD countries and became formally available in China in 2004.

Case in point

Depending on the nature of the parties involved, an advance pricing agreement may be either unilateral in kind, which involves a taxpayer and one competent tax authority, or either bilateral or multilateral in kind, involving one or more competent authorities in different tax jurisdictions.

As an example, it is assumed that a Chinese subsidiary exports its finished goods to its foreign parent firm. It is further assumed that the subsidiary claims that comparable data for such transactions from elsewhere are unavailable and that it is consequently obliged to use a 'deemed profit method' to price this cross-border transaction. If the

Chinese tax officials agree that the method adopted has produced a suitably comparable result, the tax authority will sign an advance pricing arrangement with the Chinese firm.

However, the foreign home country tax officials might find that the adopted and agreed 'deemed profit method' had inflated the prices concerned with the result of causing most profit to be retained in China. As the parent company's own domestic tax liability in respect of its Chinese subsidiary is credited by China as tax paid, it is not required to pay this income tax again. If at the time in question advance pricing agreements are not recognized between the tax administrations of the two national tax authorities concerned, the foreign tax officials might dispute the use of such a pricing method and choose to adopt the resale price method to measure the same transaction. Under this method, the profits or taxable income of the parent company would be upwardly adjusted. If the Chinese tax officials did not reciprocate by allowing a corresponding downward adjustment of the profits of the subsidiary, such an action by the foreign tax officials might result in double taxation for the multinational group. In this case, as illustrated in Figure 8.1, a bilateral or multilateral advance pricing agreement between China's State Administration of Taxation, the foreign country's tax authorities, the Chinese subsidiary, and its foreign parent firm, is required as the ultimate solution for avoiding such double taxation.

The availability of advance pricing agreements was first introduced in China in 1998 under Circular 59 of the *Tax Administration Rules and Procedures for Transactions between Related Parties*. To save the cost involved in a transfer pricing audit for both taxpayers and the tax authority, a taxpayer can secure an agreement in advance from the taxpayer's relevant tax authorities on its transfer pricing policy and the methods used for calculating prices in related party transactions.

However, Circular 59 has not provided prescribed detailed procedures for an advance pricing agreement application and the kind of information that is required from the company for such an application.

The historic first advance pricing agreement was made in a coastal city between the local tax bureau and a Taiwanese-based company. Since then over 130 unilateral advance pricing agreements have been completed, but these unilateral agreements play a limited role in preventing the evasion of tax liabilities and double taxation. On 20 September 2004, the State Administration of Taxation eventually issued the *Implementation Rules for Advance Pricing Agreements for*

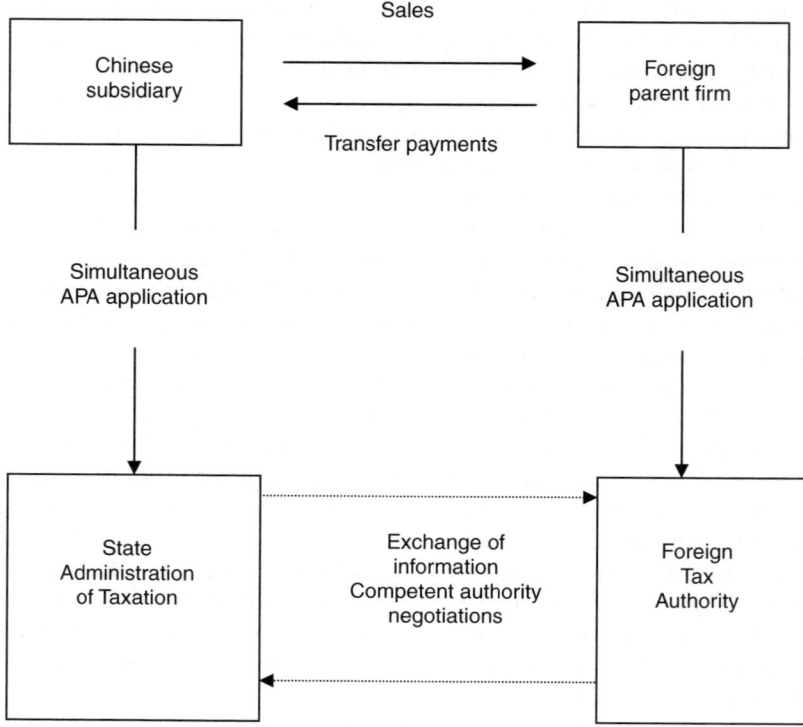

Figure 8.1 A bilateral advance pricing agreement model

Transactions between Related Parties (Guo Shui Fa [2004] No. 118, 'Implementation Rules'). The Implementation Rules explicitly recognize the possibility of bilateral and multilateral advance pricing agreements. In May 2005, China's State Administration of Taxation and Japan's National Tax Agency negotiated the first-ever advance pricing agreement for a large Japanese electronics company with subsidiaries in China. This was China's first bilateral advance pricing agreement with a foreign tax authority.

Applying for an advance pricing agreement

The Implementation Rules contain 33 articles in eight chapters under the following headings.

- Chapter 1: General principles (Articles 1–3)

- Chapter 2: Pre-file meeting (Articles 4–7)
- Chapter 3: Formal application (Articles 8–9)
- Chapter 4: Examination and evaluation (Articles 10–12)
- Chapter 5: Negotiation (Articles 13–14)
- Chapter 6: Signing the advance pricing agreement (Articles 15–17)
- Chapter 7: Execution and Monitoring (Articles 18–22)
- Chapter 8: Supplementary provisions (Articles 23–33)

An advance pricing agreement commences at the request of the taxpayer. The tax authority does not charge any fees for advance pricing proceedings. Under the Implementation Rules, the advance pricing agreement process consists of seven major stages, namely pre-filing preparations, a formal application, a review and evaluation of the application, negotiations over – and drafting of – the advance pricing agreement, signing the advance pricing agreement, its implementation, and monitoring it in practice. The details of procedures for the application of an advance pricing agreement can be illustrated as follows.

Pre-file meeting. To initiate the application process, a taxpayer must apply to the relevant tax authority for a pre-filing meeting to discuss the requirements of the proposed advance pricing agreement. During the pre-filing meeting, the local tax authority and the taxpayer together explore the feasibility of an advance pricing agreement as proposed by the taxpayer. If both parties reach an agreement to proceed with the negotiation of an advance pricing agreement, the tax authority is required to issue a written notice to the taxpayer.

At this stage, the tax authority will also discuss with the taxpayer the application procedures such as the anticipated timing for each stage, the proposal's content, a basis for its evaluation, and the duties and responsibilities for both sides. To facilitate the discussion, the taxpayer is required to provide four sets of substantial information to the tax authority, as follows.

1. A functional analysis providing a description of the respective functions performed, assets used, and risks assumed by each party to the transaction(s) under review.
2. A comparability analysis providing a comparison of a controlled transaction with an uncontrolled transaction. Controlled and uncontrolled transactions are comparable if none of the differences between the transactions could materially affect the factor being examined, or if reasonably accurate adjustments can be made to eliminate the material effects of any such differences.

3. An economic analysis to assist in the identification and valuation of the factors that contribute to the profits earned from a particular transaction. The economic value of the assets being transferred should reflect the functions performed, assets used, and risks assumed by an entity in the performance of its business activities, together with the adjustment factors affecting it, and a consideration of adjustment factors affecting the comparable information and other information of related party transactions.

Formal application. Once the local tax authority has issued a written notice confirming the feasibility of the proposed advance pricing agreement, the taxpayer is required to file a written application, generally within three months from the date when the notice was issued. The formal application should at least include the following information.

- The relevant details of related parties of the group – their corporate structure, relationships, and related party transactions
- Financial reports of three prior years, product information, including product functions, and assets involved, including tangible and intangible assets
- Related party transactions and periods to be covered under the advance pricing agreement
- Functions and risks of the relevant related parties
- Whether it will involve bilateral or multilateral advance pricing agreements with treaty countries
- Factors and assumptions considered when choosing the proposed transfer pricing method, the functional and comparable analyses that support the method selection, and the critical assumptions upon which the method depends
- Market conditions such as industrial developments, trends, and competitive market environments
- Annual forecasts and business plans for the advance pricing agreement period
- Whether relevant related parties will cooperate and provide their transactional, operational, and financial information
- Whether double taxation issues are involved
- Other issues related to domestic and international laws and tax treaties.

Review and evaluation. Upon receiving the formal application, the tax authority will analyse and evaluate the information contained within five months. The examination and evaluation work includes the following.

- Corporate operational conditions
- Functions and risks
- Comparable pricing information
- Assumptions made by the company about its future
- Transfer pricing policy and the methods used for calculating prices
- Estimates of the arm's length prices and profit range.

Negotiation and drafting of the advance pricing agreement. The next stage requires the tax authority and the taxpayer to meet, negotiate, and reach an agreement. The Implementation Rules provide that discussions with the taxpayer should be held within 30 days of the day when the tax authority reaches its conclusion during the examination and evaluation stage. If the taxpayer and the tax authority can agree on the transfer pricing methodology and associated terms and conditions, they may proceed to draft the advance pricing agreement. The draft agreement generally includes:

- Relevant details of the related companies of the group involved
- Related company transactions completed and the occurring period of the transactions
- Issue and expiry dates of the advance pricing agreement
- Transfer pricing method (s) to be used
- Clarification of terms used, such as sales revenues, sales expenses, gross profit margins, and net operating profits
- Assumptions made by the taxpayer about future conditions and operations
- Biographical and contact information on the taxpayer
- Relevant responsibilities and duties to be undertaken by the taxpayer
- Anticipated changes of circumstances that might require a revision of the advance pricing agreement
- Pending disputes involving the taxpayer with other national tax authorities or other unresolved legal liabilities and projected solutions
- Steps taken with parent company to avoid double taxation
- Anticipated events in the company's calendar
- Effective dates
- Other relevant information.

Signing of the advance pricing agreement. The taxpayer and the tax authority should sign the advance pricing agreement within 30 days after they reach an agreement on the draft advance pricing agreement. An advance pricing agreement is renewable, but the taxpayer must file a request to renew it not later than 90 days before the expiration of the initial term, and provide reliable evidence that the facts and circumstances stated in the existing advance pricing agreement have not materially changed. The tax authority should complete the examination and evaluation process and prepare a draft advance pricing agreement within 60 days of receiving the taxpayer's renewal request.

Execution and monitoring. After the signing of the advance pricing agreement, the relevant tax authority should monitor and review whether the taxpayer has complied with the conditions of that advance pricing agreement during its term. The taxpayer is also required to submit an annual advance pricing agreement compliance report to the local tax authority in charge within four months from the end of the tax year. In addition, the taxpayer is expected to report any substantial changes affecting the advance pricing agreement to the tax authority in charge, within 15 days following the date on which a change occurs.

Time limit of the advance pricing agreement. The Implementation Rules provide that the term for an advance pricing agreement may range from two to four years starting from the year after formal application. As the advance pricing agreement may take more than a year to conclude, the Implementation Rules also provide for the possibility of retrospective coverage by an advance pricing agreement up to the year of formal application. This means that a taxpayer who has signed an advance pricing agreement could be protected from transfer pricing audits for three to five years including the year of application if it properly complies with the terms of the advance pricing agreement.

Owing to the length of time taken to negotiate and conclude an advance pricing agreement, it would be cost-efficient for the taxpayer to regard an advance pricing agreement in strategic terms, and to enter into it for longer than the minimum term, especially if the business in question is of a relatively stable kind.

Confidentiality. The Implementation Rules recognize the importance of the confidential nature of the taxpayer's information. Article 25 provides that the tax authority and taxpayer have a duty in accordance with the national security laws to keep information obtained during the negotiations, examinations, and evaluations for an advance pricing agreement strictly confidential.

Article 26 provides further that where an advance pricing agreement cannot be reached between the taxpayer and the tax authority, any non-factual information obtained during the negotiation process – such as suggestions, inferences, ideas, and judgements – cannot be used by the tax authority to audit the related party's transactions previously discussed.

The above Articles are intended to encourage taxpayers to apply for advance pricing agreements by providing them with a guarantee that information they provide for advance pricing agreement applications would not be used later for transfer pricing audits against them, in the event that an advance pricing agreement could not be achieved. However, the confidentiality clauses in question only give protection to non-factual information, a definition of the precise meaning of the term non-factual being absent from the Implementation Rules.

Both the tax authority and the taxpayer have an obligation of confidentiality in relation to the advance pricing agreement information. If the negotiation fails, the tax authority is specifically prohibited from using any non-factual information – such as proposals, reasoning, notions and judgements – obtained during the failed advance pricing agreement process in any subsequent audits of the transactions that would have been covered by the abortive advance pricing agreement (Lee, Xiao, and Kuo, 2004; PricewaterhouseCoopers, 2004).

Opportunities and pitfalls in advance pricing agreement. An advance pricing agreement allows a company to negotiate the price of a product or service that will be subject to transfer pricing over a period of up to five years, rather than having to renegotiate the terms of it at the end of each year. This enables companies to plan their future tax liabilities, reduces the risks of noncompliance, and minimizes the time and cost of determining and defending their actions on a yearly basis.

In addition, under Articles 23 and 24 of the Implementation Rules, it is prescribed that advance pricing agreements should be signed as a result of a coordinated effort between different tax authorities at local and state levels, including the supervision and direct involvement of the State Administration of Taxation. This wide awareness and collaboration facilitates the opportunity for multinational enterprises with subsidiaries in multiple locations in China to apply for advance pricing agreements for their subsidiaries by negotiating directly with the State Administration of Taxation.

At present, over 130 companies have established advance pricing agreements with their relevant tax authorities. Most of these companies have been previously subjected to tax audits and subsequent income tax adjustments. Advance pricing agreements can help multinational companies to reduce the risk of a tax audit and double taxation. According to Circular 59, companies that have been audited and the recipients of imposed transfer pricing adjustments must be subject to three years of follow-up reviews subsequent to the year of audit. The handling of these follow-up reviews often demands the commitment of a good deal of managerial effort but once an advance pricing agreement is signed, follow-up reviews will not be conducted in the period covered by the advance pricing agreement.

Whilst at first sight advance pricing agreements seem to offer substantial benefits, they are not, however, without pitfalls. The negotiation process for an advance pricing agreement is invariably time consuming. The process often takes several months, at least, to reach the actual point of agreement and establish a formal advance pricing agreement. An application for an advance pricing agreement may expose the company's related party transactions to the scrutiny of the tax authorities with the risk of a leakage of trade secrets or other similar valuable information of use to the company's competitors in the market. Table 8.1 summarizes the advantages and disadvantages of advance pricing agreements.

Whilst advance pricing agreements appear at first sight to offer an escape from the trials and tribulations that might plague a company over its transfer pricing policies and enable it to avoid confrontations with the tax authorities and the imposition of penalties, the fact

Table 8.1 Advantages and disadvantages of an advance pricing agreement

Advantages	Disadvantages
1. Highest level of certainty that prices are acceptable to tax authority, therefore providing tax certainties for cross-border transactions	1. Applications for advance pricing agreements bring transactions to the attention of the tax authorities
2. Mitigated risks of being involved in a transfer pricing audit and therefore avoids the costs and burden of defending a tax audit	2. Some risk of a leakage of trade secrets or other similar valuable information
3. Multilateral advance pricing agreements reduce the risk of double taxation	3. The time consuming process involved is costly and may be unsuccessful

remains that in practice multinational companies have been less than enthusiastic in their adoption of this mechanism. Clearly, the tax authorities derive an unalloyed advantage in striking an advance pricing agreement, since it puts the company in question on the level of a known factor, guarantees the potential tax revenue for the host country, and constitutes a measure of domestic control for the host country.

One survey (Borkowski, 1996) found that, depending on the home country, the percentage of multinational enterprises with no plans to pursue advance pricing agreements with either their home or host country tax authorities ranged from 71% to 96%. Canadian multinational enterprises cited the volume of information and or documentation required as a deterrent, asserting that the cost of advance pricing agreements exceeded their benefits. German multinational enterprises ranked the volume of information required and the actual difficulty of concluding multilateral advance pricing agreements in practice as the most important deterrents. Japanese multinational enterprises were also concerned about the volume of information but they also had concerns over confidentiality. United States multinational enterprises also ranked the cost and volume of information required as the chief drawbacks to advance pricing agreements.

Summary

China has joined the other main industrial and advanced economy countries in perceiving the importance of advance pricing agreements as a means to forestall malpractice over transfer pricing involved in cross-border transactions. The volume of documentary information formally required as an accompaniment to an application for an advance pricing agreement is at first sight a daunting prospect for busy and perhaps overworked company management personnel. The compensating aspect of the time and cost needed to prepare such materials, however, is that once aggregated they can possibly be updated relatively easily as an ongoing adjunct to the company's annual accounting practice and procedures for its dealing with the tax authority, thereby serving as a long-term investment for the initial effort required.

Even so, from a company's point of view, the incessant vicissitudes of worldwide business life often demand the exemplification of versatility, adaptability, and opportunism among the characteristics of management. Whilst to be able to establish some certainties is a valuable aid to management as an antidote to complete volatility, being constrained over the pricing of transactions with a future date, and transactions that come to hand – but have not been foreseen – may not be one of them. Many, if not most, companies currently seem bent on assessing the balance of risks and costs between making an advance pricing agreement and being caught out over transfer pricing abuses, and finding in favour of the latter.

9
Contemporary Audit System

Introduction

The current Chinese transfer pricing regulations govern the administration of tax audits conducted by tax authorities on related party transactions. The rules set out detailed procedures to be followed when tax officers decide to conduct a transfer pricing audit. In general, the tax audit procedures and approaches are classified as follows.

Tax audit procedures

Identifying related party transactions and amounts. The Chinese transfer pricing rules only apply to transactions that are conducted between associated enterprises. An associated enterprise is defined as an enterprise having one of the following relationships with the taxpayer in China.

- The direct or indirect ownership or control of either or all of the Chinese company's capital, business operations, purchasing, and selling
- Sharing the common ownership or control, directly or indirectly, with a third party
- Any other associations which produce mutually beneficial outcomes.

Specifically, a company with its legal and registered home in a foreign country and an enterprise operating in China as its host country in one of the three permitted legal forms, will be considered as associated when one or more of the following conditions prevails.

- Where a foreign enterprise directly or indirectly owns 25% or more of the total share capital of the Chinese company

- Where two enterprises are directly or indirectly owned by a third enterprise holding 25% or more share capital
- Where an enterprise borrows more than 50% of its loans from another enterprise, or where an enterprise guarantees 10% or more of the loans of another enterprise
- Where one of the managing directors is, or half or more of the board of directors or executive managers of an enterprise are, appointed by another enterprise
- Where an enterprise's production can only be operated with the provision of proprietary technology owned by another enterprise
- Where the provision of raw materials, parts, and semi-finished goods used by an enterprise in production are supplied or controlled by another enterprise
- Where the sales of the commodities of an enterprise are controlled by another enterprise
- Where the production, trading activities and profits of an enterprise are effectively controlled by another enterprise having mutual benefits, such as the existence of family relationships.

To report related party transactions, a taxpayer is required to file an annual return, called the annual affiliate return, within four months of the end of the accounting year – a date which may be extended for up to 30 days on application and approval – to notify the tax authorities of the particulars relating to transactions with an associated enterprise. Separate returns should be filed for each of the associated enterprises with which a transaction has been entered into during the year. The two forms used for this purpose are

- Type A form, applicable to enterprises with a single category of affiliated party transactions
- Type B form, applicable to enterprises with multiple categories of affiliated party transactions.

Samples of these two forms are shown respectively as Tables 9.1 and 9.2.

Progressive monetary penalties are available under the law for a tax authority to fine a company which is tardy or recalcitrant over its obligations in respect of its dealings with related companies. If a foreign investment enterprise fails to file the required declaration forms to report its related party transactions within a set time, the company is subject to a penalty of up to RNB 2,000. In this case an

Table 9.1 Return for foreign investment enterprises concerning business dealings with associated companies – Type A Form

Particulars of associated enterprise	Name of the enterprise: Address: Total capital: Major business activities: Person in charge:						
Details of business dealings with associated enterprise	Type of transaction	Particulars	Date	Quality	Model/Specification	Unit pricing standard	Amount

Table 9.2 Return for foreign investment enterprises concerning business dealings with associated companies – Type B Form

Particulars of associated enterprise	Name of the enterprise: Address: Total capital: Major business activities: Person in charge: Telephone number:				
Details of business dealings with associated enterprise	Type of Transaction: Purchasing and selling Provision of funds Provision of services Use and transfer of property Provision of licenses Others	Particulars	Amount reported by company	Amount re-assessed by tax authority	Difference

extended deadline is imposed. If the company still fails to submit the forms within the new time frame set by the controlling tax bureau, it becomes subject to an additional penalty of between PE 2,000 and RNB 10,000. When a transfer pricing audit is initiated, if the company under audit provides false information or refuses to provide requested information, it is subject to a penalty of between RNB 10,000 and RNB 50,000.

Circular 59 classifies four major categories of reportable transactions with associated enterprises as follows.

- The sale, use, and transfer of tangible property including buildings, vehicles, machinery, tools and products
- The use and transfer of intangible property including land rights, copyrights, trade marks, brand names, patents, franchises and designs
- The supply of services including those for market surveys, distribution, management, administration, production techniques, maintenance, design, consultation, agency functions, scientific research, and legal and accounting work
- The provision of funds including all kinds of long-term and short-term loans, guarantees, securities, interest-bearing advances, and deferred payments.

The tax auditors are required to record the details of these transactions variously on seven standardized forms which are then acknowledged and signed by the taxpayers.

Identifying an audit target. The Chinese transfer pricing rules specify a list of the criteria for identifying potential targets for audit. These are company features that include the following.

1. Production and operational decisions controlled by associated enterprises
2. Large transaction amounts conducted with associated enterprises
3. Reported long periods of losses for more than two consecutive years
4. Lower profits or losses for an extended period, but an expanding scale of operations
5. Fluctuating profit patterns, with frequent interchanges of profits and losses
6. Transactions with associated enterprises that are established in tax havens
7. Lower profitability than the norm for enterprises in the same industry
8. Lower profit margins than other companies in the same group
9. Unreasonably high payments to associated enterprises for services rendered
10. Sudden and significant drops in profit after the termination of a preferential tax treatment period, such as a tax holiday.

It may be seen from this list of criteria that the Chinese government expects an orderly management of the affairs of a foreign investment enterprise. A company, on being eligible for a variety of fiscal and administrative concessions and advantages to assist its foundation and initial growth, must subsequently meet its just and legal obligations according to the law, in common with other companies. Failure to do so has been an endemic condition in China but the government is in the process of conducting a determined campaign to correct it. Using these criteria under the transfer pricing rules, each tax authority is required to audit at least 30% of the enterprises on the target list thereby assembled.

Office (desk) auditing. On selecting the target, tax authorities start with office (desk) auditing by reviewing working papers, including all information provided by the taxpayer. This information will include the enterprise's foundation approval documents, business and tax registration certificates, investment and operational contracts, articles of association, feasibility studies, annual financial statements, its internal audit reports, account books and vouchers, commercial contracts, and other relevant documents. The financial information the tax authorities are directed to analyse includes a company's profits or losses on sales, rates of return on investments, sales revenues, levels of costs, expenses, interest rates, and prices paid for the acquisition or use of tangible and intangible assets. The criteria of normalcy and reasonableness are applied in the examination of all these financial variables.

Field auditing. Following the office audit, a field audit will be conducted, if its desirability is indicated. Field audits are conducted by at least two personnel. A designated tax team will visit the company and conduct an on-the-spot inspection. Tax authorities are authorized to inspect an enterprise's account books and records, vouchers, sales and purchases contracts, and other relevant documents. The tax inspectors are empowered to inspect and observe the enterprise's administrative departments, workshops, and warehouses during operating hours. They may also interview relevant company employees to obtain information concerning the enterprise's pricing policies and fees standards.

Many large multinationals have established several subsidiaries in two or more locations in China. Since these related entities often have transactions with each other, cooperation among the tax bureaux in the different locations concerned is needed and important. Circular 59 (1998) specifies the procedures to be followed when the tax bureau in one location requests assistance from the tax bureau in another location during the process of a transfer pricing audit.

Onus of proof. The burden of proof regarding the arm's length price in related party transactions rests with the taxpayer. The tax authorities are not required to prove that the taxpayer intended to avoid Chinese taxation liabilities. When the tax authorities suspect that the income of a foreign investment enterprise has been concealed by a deliberate process of reducing it by non-arm's length pricing, they will require the enterprise to provide relevant information regarding transfer pricing. This will include:

- Details of transactions with affiliated enterprises and third parties, including sales and purchases, financing, the provision of human resources, the transfers of tangible and intangible assets, and the availability and use of rights
- Details bearing on factors that may contribute to the company's pricing for transactions for products and assets sold and bought, such as their amounts, locations where they were conducted, their financial forms, and the payment methods by which they were made
- Details of any other relevant matter that helped to determine the prices of transactions or helped to form the basis for charges.

Selecting an adjustment method. If the tax inspectors are sure that the buying and selling transactions between an enterprise and its associated enterprise have not been conducted in an arm's-length manner, the tax authorities will adjust the taxable income of the company according to:

- the pricing which prevails in the same or similar business activities amongst unrelated enterprises
- the profit level which may be obtained from the resale of the products to unrelated third parties
- the cost of production plus reasonable expenses and a reasonable profit margin
- any other reasonable criteria.

For transactions involving the intercompany provisions of services, loans, and the transfer of intangible assets, no particular methods are specified by the rules for determining what their arm's length results ought to be. Arm's-length prices under such circumstances are broadly referred to as any payments or receipts that a third party would agree to for the same kind of transaction.

Determining income adjustments. Adjustments made to a company's tax liabilities that have been artificially reduced by means of transfer pricing are generally restricted to the taxable profits for the year being audited and investigated. The statute of limitation for transfer pricing audits and adjustment is normally three years. In the case of exceptional adjustments that have to be made for more than three previous years, the statute of limitation can be ten years.

If a parent company does not make corresponding adjustments in its books in respect of its taxable income levels, as adjusted by the tax inspectors after the discovery of transfer price irregularities in its host country subsidiary, the concealed and unlawful income obtained by its associated enterprise in excess of the amount that would have been obtained for the same transactions with unrelated companies is regarded as a dividend payment. The deemed dividend is not entitled to the privilege of exemption from income tax. If the income obtained by the associated company is in the form of interest or royalties, there will be no recovery of the withholding tax already paid on the excessive interest or royalties.

Revised assessments and the appeals procedure. If the taxpayer does not agree with the transfer pricing adjustments made by the tax authority, he can appeal to the tax authorities with additional supporting documentation within 60 days for an administrative appeal. A decision on the appeal must be made within 60 days. Tax authorities may re-evaluate their adjustments and consult further with the taxpayer. Following this and its reconsideration of the case, the relevant tax authority will issue a notice of payment for its assessed transfer pricing adjustment. With the issue of this written notice, the outcome is generally regarded as being final. If the taxpayer is still not satisfied with the decision, he may start legal proceedings in the court within 15 days of receiving notice of the decision.

However, in practice, such litigation is rare in China. Three reasons for this fact generally prevail. In the first place companies are reluctant to antagonize their tax authority further, once their misdemeanors over tax avoidance or evasion by means of transfer pricing have been exposed, since they subsequently need to co-exist in amicable relations with the tax authority in the future Secondly, in the absence of specialized tax courts in China, Chinese courts do not have a general power of statutory interpretation. The tax authorities are often authorized both to administer and interpret the implementing tax regulations that constitute the bulk of the tax legislation. Courts are anyway cognizant of the endemic practice of transfer pricing abuse and are likely to uphold the findings of the tax authority, provided they are convinced that the latter's investigations and calculations have been properly and accurately conducted as prescribed by the established regulations. Thirdly, the cost of litigation in several dimensions, not least on account of the extended time for its realization and fulfilment, is normally a powerful deterrent.

Tax audit structure and practice

The latest obtainable figures disclose that until recently in China there were 798,861 tax officials in total. Of these, 439,374 (55%) obtained a university or college education, 98,347 having a bachelor's or higher degree, accounting for 12.31% of the overall total. At present, altogether about 300 officers appear to be devoted exclusively to anti-tax avoidance activities, but it is believed that this number has been recently increased and will be increased further in the future.

Most tax bureaux at city and provincial levels have established anti-avoidance offices exclusively to deal with transfer pricing issues. Gansu, Ningxia, Qinghai, and Tibet Autonomous Regions, however, are the exception. Compared with the other areas of China, these Autonomous Regions attract few foreign direct investments. Transfer pricing, therefore, is not regarded as a prominent issue for the tax authorities in these areas.

Each year, the tax authorities in China conduct approximately 5,000 desk audits and about 1,000 field audits. In view of the size of the task, following the huge rise in the number of foreign investment enterprises and the growth of their cross-border transactions following China's admission to the World Trade Organization, the Chinese tax authorities are enhancing the impact of their inevitably disproportionate resources and capability for tax collection by increasingly resorting to the employment of transfer pricing audits.

During the period 1991 to 2001, the tax authorities audited up to 18,000 foreign investment enterprises and foreign enterprises for their related party transactions. The 6,000 audited cases actually carried through to completion resulted in an assessed additional taxable income of RMB 15 billion, and corresponding corporate income tax charges totalling RMB 1.8 billion. The enterprises audited were only a small proportion of foreign investment enterprises operating in China, and most of the enterprises audited were small in scale.

Operational data

Data on the operational practice and achievements of four state tax bureaux were collected for the purposes of this book. Two of these are located in a major coastal city which has provincial status. The other two are in a large inland city, the capital city of its province. In the following accounts of the operations of these tax authorities, these two cities are respectively referred to as City A and City B.

The two Municipal State Tax Bureaux in City A are entirely responsible for the supervision of tax assessment and collection in their respective large areas, and the conduct of investigations into tax avoidance and evasion as necessary, subject to the National State Tax Bureau. Each in turn supervises a large number of County State Tax Bureaux and a few District State Tax Bureaux, each of which in its assigned sub-area implements the day-by-day routine work of collection, and which selects foreign investment enterprises to audit. In 2002, foreign investment enterprises contributed about 21.8% of City A's total tax revenue. One of these County State Tax Bureaux, subject to the Municipal State Tax Bureaux, has twelve departments, one of which is designated 'Foreign Tax Department' and is responsible for conducting transfer pricing audits throughout its area of the city.

In City B, the two Inland Provincial State Tax Bureaux, guided by goals established by the National State Tax Bureaux, are similarly responsible for the supervision of tax assessment and collection, and the conduct of investigations into tax avoidance and evasion as necessary throughout the province. In the province in question in 2002, 51 foreign investment enterprises that had conducted business transactions with their associated enterprises abroad were audited. As a result, the transfer prices of 36 foreign investment enterprises were adjusted, resulting in an increase of taxable income of RMB 163.18 million. Eight foreign investment enterprises were adjusted by adopting the comparable uncontrolled price method, two were adjusted by adopting the resale price method, 17 were adjusted by adopting the cost plus method, one was adjusted by adopting the profit split method, and eight were adjusted by adopting the deemed profit method. These adjustments resulted in overall profits being posted by the tax authorities for nine foreign investment enterprises for 2002 – sufficient to make up for their accumulated losses brought forward from the previous year, and which, in turn, resulted in increased tax revenues of RMB 46.34 million.

The four tax authorities were asked to comment on the existing transfer pricing auditing systems. Three tax authorities considered their auditing systems to be 'moderately effective'. One tax authority was not satisfied with its auditing system and considered the auditing system to be 'ineffective'. The tax authorities pointed out that the most common problem encountered in the implementation of their transfer pricing tax audits was 'the difficulty in obtaining relevant pricing information of foreign investment enterprises with their related companies outside China.'

Another problem was the difficulty of determining the pricing of intercompany transfers of intangible goods, such as research and marketing. 'The transfer of intangibles is particularly difficult for the arm's length principle to deal with as finding useful comparable data is very hard. The measures of such transactions such as payments for intellectual property rights, know-how, and other payments of a similar nature, cause the biggest problem for us.' In addition, the tax authorities face difficulties in determining inter-group services and calculating the justifiable fees for them. 'It is often difficult for us to find a comparable price for such services provided to a foreign investment enterprise by its parent company abroad. If we deem that the fees charged are not comparable with the fees which are charged by arm's length enterprises, adjustments may be made, accordingly, for tax purposes.'

Since China's entrance into the World Trade Organization in December 2001, the Chinese government has cut customs tariffs on several occasions, and has indicated that they will be cut further. To protect its tax revenue base at the same time, the Chinese tax authority has been actively strengthening its transfer pricing legislation and investigative activities.

Transfer pricing case. The following is a transfer pricing audit case in 1997. A Sino-Korean, Wholly Owned Subsidiary was established in 1992. This company manufactures leather clothing in China and exports its products to overseas markets. The firm's production and operations are wholly controlled by its parent company in Korea. Since opening the business, the company progressively expanded its scale of operations, its sales volumes constantly increasing, but reported cumulative losses of RMB 83 million. The tax officials detected that the parent company supplied the orders and raw materials, the Chinese subsidiary processing and making a variety of leather clothes according to the requirements of its parent company. Instead of paying fees on the basis of the processing costs and expenses, the parent company paid fixed processing fees to the subsidiary according to their advance contracts. The company's overall expenses rate was around 10% but the parent only paid 6% as processing fees. In addition, the tax officials found that the sales prices of the company to the parent company were low.

From 1992 to 1996, the subsidiary's average gross profit margin was only 2.3% – lower than that for companies in the same industry. The tax authority considered that the company's sales prices to its parent company were lower than the corresponding prices in the open market. Acting according to the Income Tax Law of the People's Republic of China concerning Foreign Investment Enterprises and Foreign Enterprises, and the Law of the People's Republic of China concerning Tax Collection and Administration, the tax authority used the comparable uncontrolled price method to adjust the company's profit margin. This resulted in an increased charge of corporate income tax of RMB 301,974.07. The company accepted the adjustment and paid the income tax on demand in due course.

Summary

The vigilance of the tax authorities in China is compromised by the size of the country, regional variations in the number of staff available, and the sheer number of commercial activities operated by foreign firms. There has been an increase of audit activity by the tax authorities, however, acting along the well-defined lines laid down at national level for the investigation of transfer pricing irregularities and making the necessary corrective adjustments to them. This chapter has outlined the procedural steps taken as standard audit conduct, summarized in Figure 9.1.

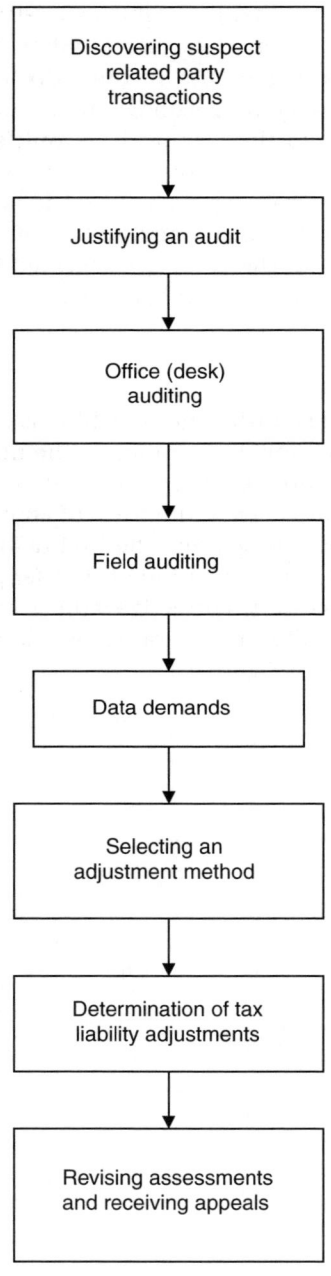

Figure 9.1 Steps in the procedure for conducting a transfer pricing audit

Part III
Experience of Audit

10
Foreign Company Practice

Introduction

A global survey conducted in 2003 by Ernst and Young (2003) revealed that 86% of the respondent companies considered transfer pricing to be the most important international tax issue facing them. Forty per cent of respondent firms reported that they had been subject to transfer pricing adjustments, suffering double taxation.

In the same year, as reported in Li and Paisey (2005), a survey of 47 foreign owned Chinese subsidiaries was conducted with a view to a study of their transfer pricing practices. The findings of this research provided additional knowledge of transfer pricing tax auditing practices in China. Additional findings from this research and analyses of it provide the data and discussion presented below.

Company data

Home country/region of parent company. Table 10.1 shows the home country/region of parent companies which have subsidiary companies operating in China. It covers a wide range of nationalities. Of all the countries/regions concerned, however, Hong Kong, the United States, Japan, and Taiwan are by far most likely to be the home of parent companies which have subsidiaries operating in China. Together these countries/regions account for 61.7% of the total.

Volume of intercompany international transfers. The levels of intercompany transfers as a percentage of total company transfers for these companies are shown in Table 10.2. Total company transfers means a company's worldwide transactions with related or unrelated parties. Nine companies (19.1%) have intercompany transfers of less

116 Transfer Pricing Audits in China

Table 10.1 The home country/region of the companies surveyed

Country/region	Number of companies	Percentage
Hong Kong	10	21.3
United States	8	17
Japan	6	12.8
Taiwan	5	10.6
France	3	6.4
Korea	3	6.4
Singapore	3	6.4
United Kingdom	2	4.3
Germany	1	2.1
Sweden	1	2.1
The Netherlands	1	2.1
Italy	1	2.1
Virgin Islands	1	2.1
Macao	1	2.1
Thailand	1	2.1
Total	47	100

Table 10.2 Intercompany transfers as percentages of total company transfers

Range	Number of firms	Percentage
Less than 5%	9	19.1
6% to 20%	12	25.5
21% to 50%	13	27.7
51% to 70%	6	12.8
71% to 85%	4	8.5
More than 85%	3	6.4
Total	47	100

Table 10.3 The nature and frequency of intercompany transfers of tangible goods, intangible goods, services, and finances

Assets transferred	Always	Often	Sometimes	Rarely	Never
Tangible goods	17	12	11	3	2
Intangible goods	5	3	8	13	13
Services	9	5	15	11	3
Finances	5	11	5	11	10

Note. Some of the 47 companies declined to provide information

than 5% of their total company transfers. Three respondents (6.4%) have a volume of intercompany transfers which amounts to more than 85% of their total company transfers.

The nature and frequency of intercompany transfers. The nature and frequency of their intercompany transfers are shown in Table 10.3. It may be seen that transfers of tangible goods and services are the most common activities.

Transfer pricing methods used. The respondents were asked to state their preferred method or methods used in calculating/adjusting the prices of their transactions with their related parties outside China. The responses are shown in Table 10.4. These methods can be grouped according to two principles. Transaction-based methods include comparable uncontrolled price (CUP), resale price (RP), and cost plus (CPL). Profit-based methods include comparable profit (CP) and profit split (PS). Transaction-based methods compare prices or gross margins, whereas profit-based methods compare net profits. The transactional net margin method (TNM) deals with how prices are set while the comparable profit method requires an arm's length result. It is considered that in practice there is little to distinguish these two pricing methods from each other. In this book, the comparable profit method may be taken to include the transactional net margin method.

The choice of pricing methods by companies depends on the different types of international transfers involved. The most frequently used pricing method by Chinese firms is cost plus, a method which

Table 10.4 The legally oriented transfer pricing methods used in order of frequency

Transfer pricing methods	Number of firms	Percentage
Transaction-based		
Cost plus	21	29.2
Comparable uncontrolled price	17	23.6
Resale price	7	9.7
Subtotal for transaction-based methods	45	62.5
Profit-based		
Comparable profit	19	26.39
Profit split	6	8.3
Subtotal for profit-based methods	25	34.72
Others	2	2.8
Total – all methods*	72	100

Note: *Some companies used more than one transfer pricing method.

Table 10.5 Transfer pricing methods used in practice according to industry in order of frequency

Industry	CPL	CUP	RP	CP	PS	Others	Total
Manufacturing	10	8	4	9	5	1	37
Wholesale & retail trades	7	8	1	7	0	0	23
Services	2	1	1	1	1	0	6
Construction	1	0	1	2	0	0	4
Agriculture	1	0	0	0	0	1	2
Total	21	17	7	19	6	2	72

Table 10.6 Transfer pricing methods used by the respondent firms of different nationalities in order of frequency

Transfer pricing methods	Hong Kong	Japan	Taiwan	United States	Others
Cost plus	6	3	3	4	5
Comparable uncontrolled price	3	4	3	1	6
Resale price	1	1	1	0	4
Comparable profit	3	2	2	2	5
Profit split	1	1	1	1	2
Others	0	0	0	2	0

Note: Some companies used more than one transfer pricing method.

accounted for 29.2% of the respondent companies. The preference for this method may reflect the fact that many of the firms in the survey are engaged in manufacturing industries. It could also be due to the ease with which it can be used as a measure. Nineteen companies use the comparable profit method, seventeen use the comparable uncontrolled price method, and seven companies use the resale price method. The profit split method is used by six firms. Two companies used other methods – 'global formulary apportionment' and 'going-rate pricing', which are not specified by the State Administration of Taxation. The divergence of the methods used by these companies from the recommended methods could be as a result of the unique nature of their intercompany transactions.

Table 10.5 classifies transfer pricing methods used according to the industry. It can be observed that the cost plus method is the most predominantly used method in the manufacturing industry. One manufacturing firm and one agricultural firm use other methods not specified by the State Administration of Taxation. Although the resale price method is generally considered to be the most suitable transfer pricing method for use in the distribution industry, only one in 23 companies engaged in wholesale and retail trading are using this method.

A nationality breakdown of transfer pricing methods used by the respondents is given in Table 10.6. It can be seen that Hong Kong and United States firms tend to use the cost plus method, while there is no comparably strong tendency in preference for Japanese, Taiwanese, and other companies.

Transfer pricing methods used

The respondent firms were further asked about transfer pricing methods used from a business policy viewpoint. This question was directed at uncovering whether cost-based or market-based prices were in operation. Table 10.7 shows that 34.1% of the Chinese firms use cost-based methods and 65.9% use market-based methods for the combined groups. Chinese companies tend to use market oriented methods. As for the use of the individual pricing methods, 'full market price' (8 or 18.2%) and 'negotiation based on costs' (8 or 18.2%) are

Table 10.7 Transfer pricing methods used by the respondent companies

Methods	Number of firms	Percentage
Cost-Based Methods		
Full actual cost	7	15.9
Full plus fixed profit	3	6.8
Variable plus fixed contribution	3	6.8
Full standard cost	1	2.3
Variable standard cost	1	2.3
Variable actual cost	0	0
Subtotal for Cost-Based Methods	15	34.1
Market-Based Methods		
Full market price	8	18.2
Negotiation based on costs	8	18.2
Negotiation based on market price	7	15.9
Adjusted market price	6	13.6
Subtotal for Market-Based Methods	29	65.9
Total – all Methods	44	100

Table 10.8 Reported transfer pricing tax audits

Response	Hong Kong	Japan	Taiwan	USA	Others	Total
Audit	6	2	2	4	1	15
No audit	4	4	3	4	15	30
Total	10	6	5	8	16	45

most commonly used by respondent companies. Following these in descending order of frequency of use are 'full actual cost' (7 or 15.9%), 'negotiation based on market prices' (7 or 15.9%), 'adjusted market price' (6 or 13.6%), 'full plus fixed profit' (3 or 6.8%), 'variable plus fixed contribution' (3 or 6.8%), 'full standard cost' (1 or 2.3%), and 'variable standard cost' (1 or 2.3%).

Transfer pricing tax audit. The respondents were asked if their companies had been subject to a transfer pricing tax audit. Their responses are shown in Table 10.8. Fifteen companies (18% of respondents to the question) have been subject to transfer pricing tax audits. The table shows that Hong Kong-based firms have experienced a higher rate of transfer pricing audits than firms from other countries. In view of Hong Kong's generous tax system and low income tax rate of 16%, Hong Kong-based firms may have the incentive to try to minimize their tax liabilities by artificially shifting profits from abroad to Hong Kong through transfer pricing mechanisms. This singular advantage probably generates the prior interest of the tax authorities and leads to a higher rate of audit of Hong Kong owned subsidiaries than that imposed on companies from other home countries.

Factors affecting transfer pricing

Because of their widespread international operations, multinational enterprises are exposed to a greater variety of organizational and environmental 'disturbances' than domestic enterprises. The range and severity of these factors differ substantially from country to country and may be imperfectly monitored and understood. In practice, the way managers perceive the conditions created by these factors is likely to have a great impact on how they determine their transfer pricing policies. The fundamental organizational and environmental factors most likely to influence a company's pricing behaviour may include, but are not limited to the following (Li and Paisey, 2005).

Comply with tax law and regulations. Complying with tax law and government regulations plays a significant role in the formulation of multinational transfer prices. A number of legal-related variables such as compliance with tax and custom regulations, anti-dumping and antitrust legislation, and financial reporting rules of the host countries, are important factors in multinational transfer pricing decisions. Such governmental countermeasures may constrain the transfer pricing manipulation behaviour of multinational enterprises and, therefore, force them to use market prices for internal dealings.

Corporate profit of the subsidiary. The arbitrary movement of profits from a foreign subsidiary by means of transfer pricing to enhance overall corporate profitability, may affect the measured profitability of the subsidiary concerned, thereby distorting the perceivable professional performance of its managers. Such managers of foreign subsidiaries may have a strong incentive to establish their own good profit records and, therefore, would be disinclined to establish prices that reduced the profits of their own companies. In designing transfer pricing systems, local managers are likely to seek to balance the interests of the profit to the multinational group as a whole with that of the corporate profit of the subsidiary.

Rates of customs duties. In industrialized nations, as in developing countries, import and export duties serve as protective devices rather than as a vehicle for meeting distributive objectives. Consequently, import duties in many countries tend to be substantially higher than they used to be. The tariffs for which a company may be liable, therefore, can be reduced by making transfers of their assets at an arbitrarily low price. The lower the price at which goods can be transferred, the lower the tariff payments which have to be paid on them. A multinational company needs to have an inducement whereby the parent company underprices goods by using transfer pricing means to gain fiscal savings at the expense of the host government. At the same time it needs to be recognized that where high tariffs and high income tax rates go hand in hand, a company that escapes liabilities over import charges may then lose its gains to the resultant heavier income tax dues.

Competitive position of subsidiary. Multinational enterprises enter foreign markets by establishing subsidiaries or branches. Frequently, transfer pricing is used to facilitate the penetration of foreign markets by an overseas subsidiary, or to support an infant subsidiary abroad in its competition with local firms. In these cases, the parent company may temporarily under price any assets transferred to the subsidiary to provide support for it in another country where it wants to increase its market share.

Overall profit to multinational group. The maximization of global profit is a major objective for multinational enterprises. This objective can be partly facilitated by shifting income from higher rate to lower rate tax jurisdictions to minimize total tax liabilities and thereby maximize after-tax profits. However, while aiming to achieve this objective, multinational enterprises also have to deal with other competing – and sometimes directly conflicting – factors, such as governmental regulations, currency fluctuations, and foreign exchange controls and risks. Their ability to balance these competing factors in their choice of transfer pricing methods is crucial – and likely to determine the level of overall profits that they are able to achieve.

Maintenance of cash flows. A multinational enterprise may prefer to accumulate its funds to meet current financial needs to ensure that there are sufficient cash reserves to cope with its financial commitments and to meet unforeseen demands, thus ensuring financial stability. Transfer pricing may then be employed as a means of shifting funds into a subsidiary. For example, a local manager may feel pressure to maintain adequate cash flows in the subsidiary. Transfer pricing manipulation may be encouraged by the cash flow requirements of the company.

Good relations with host government. The practice by multinational enterprises of shifting profits out of host countries has attracted considerable attention from governments. Concerned about the potential adverse effects on their economies, the tax authorities of host countries have adopted an increasingly aggressive attitude towards the audit of multinational transfer pricing practices, and have placed some economic restrictions on their operations. These actions can impose intense pressures upon companies. If disputes with local tax officials arise, they can be costly to foreign subsidiaries. Consequently, multinational enterprises have realized the importance of maintaining positive relations with host governments. In justifying their transfer pricing methods, some subsidiaries are even willing to sacrifice some profits by transfer pricing to satisfy host governments. Their end purpose is to forestall any government action that may have potentially longer-term detrimental effects.

Performance evaluation. Corporate policies regarding transfer pricing for tax evasion purposes may be in conflict with the performance evaluation of subsidiary managers. For example, arbitrarily shifting profits from a foreign subsidiary by transfer pricing means –

while enhancing overall corporate profitability – may affect the measured profitability of that subsidiary and, in turn, distort the performance records of the subsidiary's managers. Performance is frequently evaluated on the basis of net income and return on investment. To resolve this conflict, multinational enterprises often separate managerial performance from that of the subsidiary's overall performance. Another alternative is to set a 'fair' transfer price – an intercompany price that managers can perceive as equity in performance evaluation, based on an externally established market price.

Restrictions on repatriation of income. Limits imposed on the remittance of profits abroad create a strong inducement for a multinational enterprise to use the transfer pricing mechanism. In some less developed countries, notably those that often suffer from balance-of-payment problems, governments may introduce a number of regulations or policies to restrict profit and capital repatriations. When foreign subsidiaries face the difficulties of profit remittances to their home countries, they may plan to circumvent such constraints through the use of transfer pricing. In this case, the parent company can artificially raise its sale prices to the foreign subsidiary to avoid the restrictions on the remittances. In addition, transfer pricing may be used to minimize withholding tax on dividends. By artificially setting high prices for transferred-in goods, cash is funneled to the parent company from the swollen sales prices. This leaves less profit in the subsidiary's country, thereby reducing the need to transfer funds to the parent company through dividends.

Existence of local partner. Multinational enterprises sometimes conduct business in foreign environments through joint ventures for political, legal or cultural reasons. For example, some host governments in developing countries require that a local firm must be a partner in the business venture of a foreign-based company. Multinational enterprises themselves may use the strategy of engaging local involvements for bridging cultural gaps and fostering cultural understanding. In most arrangements of this type, both sides – foreign investors (subsidiaries) and local partners in joint ventures – share the profits, costs and management responsibilities. This means that a foreign investor has only a part profit share, the rest being distributed to the local partner who has legal rights to a fair share of the profit of the business. To restrict the profits accruing to the partner, and in return, to increase its own interest and benefit, the parent company has high motivation to shift profits out of the joint venture by transfer pricing manoeuvres.

Foreign currency exchange controls. In some developing nations, foreign exchange is stringently constrained by governments, the local currencies being only semi-convertible. In this situation, a multinational enterprise faces problems in converting profits into the currency of the home country. Moreover, when the local currency unit is devalued, exchange losses may rise. Companies usually view exchange uncertainties as their most pervasive risk in foreign environments. In most cases, they tend to hedge this risk through changes in the timing of payments, that is, by leading (anticipatory moves) or lagging (delaying techniques). For example, a buying company may pay a selling company before the due date (leading) and thereby anticipate a fall in the currency of the buyer's country. In this way, an exchange loss may be averted. Transfer pricing practices can enhance the exchange-risk-avoiding strategies of leading or lagging. A company faced with exchange rate risks can use a higher transfer price to move funds out of countries with weak currencies into countries with strong ones. In this particular case, the perceived exchange loss risk may induce the parent company to transfer profits out of the host country through overpricing.

Political and social pressures. Political and social pressures as determinants appear to be related to some of the aforementioned factors. Volatile fluctuations in the value of currencies, high inflation rates, foreign exchange controls, and restrictions on remittances, increase financial risks and uncertainty for a multinational enterprise. A lack of political stability can increase the political risks for a company's foreign subsidiaries. In some developing countries the threat of expropriation and nationalization is often a concern for multinational enterprises. All these factors impose political and social pressures on business operations. Consequently, companies tend to transfer profits out of the disadvantageous host country to avoid these risks. In some countries, labour unions exercise a significant influence. They may impose pressures on subsidiaries to raise wages for local workers in response to the perceived high operating earnings of foreign firms. To nullify claims for higher wages by local labour unions, the parent company may overprice transferred assets to reduce the profits of its subsidiaries (Belkaoui, 1991). In conclusion, a host country that tries to control or limit the activities of multinationals may be considered an undesirable place for retaining high profits with safety in the long term. A multinational's subsidiaries may use transfer pricing mechanisms to send profits abroad.

Differences in income tax rates. Disparities in tax rates across countries create an obvious and powerful incentive for the member units of a multinational enterprise to try to minimize tax liabilities in the home or host countries, but, in turn, to maximize joint profits within the enterprise as a whole. This effect can be accomplished by artificially shifting taxable income from affiliates which operate in high-tax jurisdictions to their related subsidiaries in low-tax jurisdictions – an operation which results in the overall reduction of total worldwide tax payments which the multinational enterprise actually makes.

Import restrictions. When goods are transferred from a parent company to an overseas subsidiary in a foreign country, the host government may impose anti-dumping charges on the multinational company to protect its home industries against the export of the excess production of companies in other countries. Dumping is recognized as taking place when goods are sold at a lower price for export than for domestic consumption in the exporting country under comparable conditions of sale. In this case the parent company may overprice to escape charges of anti-dumping practices.

Tax authority transfer pricing audits. A great number of developed countries have enacted sophisticated tax regulations and employ highly qualified professional tax experts to deal with transfer pricing practices. In contrast, although they may have become aware of the losses of tax revenues as a result of these practices, the governments of developing countries find it difficult to deal with the problem as they lack the institutional framework and administrative expertise to analyse the complex set of factors at work. They may even find it difficult to detect the practices at all. When they are able to do so they simply do not have the resources to control and monitor them effectively. Hence, the threat of transfer pricing auditing by tax authorities might not be taken seriously as an imminent and realistic threat by the multinationals operating in developing countries.

Royalty restrictions. Multinational enterprises are organizations which have one or more subsidiaries operating in foreign markets. Internal prices are often set for the transfer of intangible goods – such as research and development costs and intellectual property – from the foreign subsidiaries to their parent companies. Many host governments have imposed some restrictions on the amount of royalty or management fees the local subsidiaries can pay to their parent companies abroad. To avoid governmental royalty restrictions and, in turn, to facilitate the local subsidiary's ability to remit more profits overseas, in such cases, the parent company may set a high transfer price on goods sold to the subsidiary.

Pricing controls of host governments. In some industries, host governments control prices in relation to the costs and profits of foreign companies, requiring that all price increases be approved by government agencies in advance. High import prices can reduce profits and increase costs, thereby justifying increased prices. In this case, the parent company may allow its subsidiaries to record a low profit by overpricing to resist the introduction of price controls.

Organizational and environmental variable rankings

The rankings of the importance of all these organizational and environmental variables by the respondents of different nationalities are given in Table 10.9. The rankings of their importance are determined by the mean scores of the variables. Multinational companies operating in foreign countries consider compliance with host legal regulations as an important variable in the formulation of their transfer pricing policies. Despite national differences, firms based in Hong Kong, Japan, Taiwan, and the United States, commonly select 'comply with tax law and regulations' as a very important variable.

Table 10.9 Rankings of the importance of the organizational and environmental variables for transfer pricing policy decisions by respondent firms of different nationalities

Variables	Hong Kong	Japan	Taiwan	USA	Others
Comply with tax law and regulations	1	2	2	1	5
Corporate profit of the subsidiary	2	3	2	3	2
Rates of customs duties	3	4	5	3	4
Competitive position of the subsidiary	3	4	3	4	3
Overall profit to multinational group	3	1	1	4	1
Maintenance of cash flows	4	5	4	2	7
Good relations with host government	5	5	4	4	14
Performance evaluation	6	5	4	5	6
Restrictions on repatriation of income	7	4	6	5	10
Existence of local partner	7	6	4	8	9
Foreign currency exchange controls	8	4	6	6	13
Political and social pressures	8	7	9	11	15
Differences in income tax rates	9	3	6	3	8
Import restrictions	9	7	6	10	12
Tax authority transfer pricing audits	10	5	8	7	11
Royalty restrictions	10	6	7	9	16
Price controls of host government	11	6	7	8	9

Three variables, 'corporate profit of the subsidiary', 'overall profit to multinational group', and 'competitive position of the subsidiary', are consistently given high ratings among the seventeen listed environmental variables by all national groups. This is not surprising since profitability has always remained a major objective of transfer pricing for multinational enterprises, if not always the only one. Their competitive positions in foreign markets are vital to their survival.

Compared with the other national groups, Japanese companies place greater importance on 'tax authority transfer pricing audits'. This is natural in view of the fact that Japanese-owned companies are patently subject to more scrutiny and are more readily audited than others by host country tax authorities in the world as a matter of record. They must therefore recognize the importance of 'tax authority transfer pricing audits' as a foremost element in formulating their transfer pricing policies.

Statistical references

Logistic Regression Analysis. To investigate the significance of organizational and environmental variables for the choice of transfer pricing methods in a multivariate setting, a logit model was developed as follows.

ITPM $= \beta_0 + \beta_1 SIZE + \beta_2 INDUSTRY + \beta_3 TANGIBLE + \beta_4 INTANGIBLE + \beta_5 SERVICES + \beta_6 FINANCE + \beta_7 GOVERNMENT + \beta_8 CORPORATE + \beta_9 LEGAL + \varepsilon$

Where:

ITPM = International transfer pricing method. The dependent variable assumes the value of 1 if prices are cost-based, 0 if market-based.

SIZE = Company size A value of 1 is assigned if total sales are less than $20m, 2 if $20m to $100m, 3 if $101 m to $200m, 4 if $201m to $500m, 5 if $501m to $800m, and 6 if more than $800m.

INDUSTRY = Industry type. A value of 1 is assigned if it is in manufacturing and 0 if it is in another type of industry.

TANGIBLE = Transfer of tangible goods. A value of 1 is assigned if transfer of tangible goods never happened, 2 if rarely, 3 if often, and 4 if always.

INTANGIBLE = Transfer of intangible goods. A value of 1 is assigned if transfer of intangible goods never happened, 2 if rarely, 3 if often, and 4 if always.

SERVICES = Transfer of services. A value of 1 is assigned if transfer of services never happened, 2 if rarely, 3 if often, and 4 if always.

FINANCE = Transfer of finance. A value of 1 is assigned if transfer of finance never happened, 2 if rarely, 3 if often, and 4 if always.

GOVERNMENT = Government restrictions variable. Arranged in descending order of factor loading, the following items loaded on the Government variable: 1. import restrictions; 2. price controls of host government; 3. royalty restrictions; 4. foreign currency exchange controls; 5. restrictions on repatriation of income; 6. political and social pressure. A value of 1 is assigned if it is not important, 2 if slightly important, 3 if important, 4 if very important, and 5 if extremely important.

CORPORATE = Corporate competitive position variable. Arranged in descending order of factor loading, the following items loaded on the Corporate variable: 1. competitive position of the subsidiary; 2. performance evaluation; 3. corporate profit of the subsidiary; 4. existence of local partner; 5. overall profit to multinational group; 6. good relations with host government; 7. maintenance of cash flows. A value of 1 is assigned if it is not important, 2 if slightly important, 3 if important, 4 if very important, and 5 if extremely important.

LEGAL = Legal and tax variable. Arranged in descending order of factor loading, the following items loaded on the Legal variable: 1. comply with tax law and regulations; 2. differences in income tax rates; 3. tax authority transfer pricing audits; 4. rates of customs duties. A value of 1 is assigned if it is not important, 2 if slightly important, 3 if important, 4 if very important, and 5 if extremely important.

The results of the logistic regression analysis of the significance of the organizational and environmental variables from the data of the respondent foreign investment enterprises are shown in Table 10.10. The model classified cost-based transfer pricing methods with 78.57% accuracy and market-based transfer pricing methods with

Table 10.10 Logistic regression analysis of the significance of the organizational and environmental variables

Panel A: Overall results	Predicted sign	Coefficient	Standard Error	Significance
Intercept	+/−	−11.6171	5.2207	.0261**
SIZE	+/−	.7624	.4023	.0581*
INDUSTRY	+/−	−2.4314	1.4845	.1014
TANGIBLE GOODS	+/−	2.6066	1.0390	.0121**
INTANGIBLE GOODS	+/−	−.8164	.6403	.2023
SERVICES	+/−	.7799	.5385	.1475
FINANCE	+/−	−1.2556	.5858	.0321**
GOVERNMENT	+	.5741	.2328	.0137**
CORPORATE	+/−	.1602	.1406	.2548
LEGAL	−	−.8117	.3196	.0111**

87.50% accuracy. The overall predictive accuracy of 84.81% indicates a good fit for the model. Of the nine variables used in the logit model, the Size variable is statistically significant at the 10% level, the Tangible, Finance, Government, and Legal variables are statistically significant at the 5% level. The results indicate that the Size, Tangible, Finance, Government, and Legal variables are the most important factors in determining which transfer pricing policies will be employed by foreign investment enterprises in China. The signs (+/−) of coefficients are positive for the Size, Tangible, and Government variables, while they are negative for the Finance and Legal variables.

Test of Size

Table 10.10 shows that the Size variable is statistically significant at the 10% level and positively related to cost-based transfer pricing. This indicates that the larger the size of a foreign investment enterprise, the more likely it is that cost-based transfer pricing was used.

Test of Industry

Table 10.10 shows that the Industry variable, while statistically insignificant, is negatively associated with cost-based transfer pricing methods. Therefore, although foreign investment enterprises in manufacturing industry may prefer market-based transfer pricing, it cannot be concluded that the Industry variable is the driving factor in establishing market-based transfer prices.

Test of Tangible Goods

Table 10.10 shows that the Tangible variable is statistically significant at the 5% level and positively related to cost-based transfer pricing. This indicates that the more heavily a foreign investment enterprise engaged in intercompany transfers of tangible goods, the more likely it is that cost-based transfer pricing was used.

Test of Intangible Goods

Table 10.10 shows that the Intangible variable, while statistically insignificant, is negatively associated with cost-based transfer pricing methods. Therefore, it cannot be concluded that the Intangible variable is a significant factor in a foreign investment enterprise's decision to use a market-based transfer pricing.

Test of Services

Table 10.10 shows that the Service variable, while statistically insignificant, is positively associated with cost-based transfer pricing methods. Therefore, it cannot be concluded that the Service variable is a significant factor in a foreign investment enterprise's decision to use a cost-based transfer pricing.

Test of Finance

Table 10.10 shows that the Financing variable is statistically significant at the 5% level and negatively related to cost-based transfer pricing. This indicates that the more heavily a foreign investment enterprise engaged in intercompany transfers of financing, the more likely it is that market-based transfer pricing was used.

Test of Government

Table 10.10 shows that the Government variable is statistically significant at the 5% level and positively related to cost-based transfer pricing. This implies that foreign investment enterprises may use cost-based transfer pricing to circumvent economic restrictions imposed by the Chinese government.

Test of Corporate

Table 10.10 shows that the Corporate variable, while statistically insignificant, is positively associated with cost-based transfer pricing methods. Therefore, it cannot be concluded that the Corporate variable was a driving factor in a foreign investment enterprise's decision to use a cost-based transfer pricing.

Test of Legal

Table 10.10 shows that the Legal variable is statistically significant at the 5% level and negatively related to cost-based transfer pricing. This indicates that foreign investment enterprises may use market-based transfer pricing to comply with the laws and regulations of the Chinese government.

Advance pricing agreement. The results of this survey also showed that multinational firms typically appeared to be uninterested in participating in advance pricing agreement programmes. As shown in Table 10.11, only one Hong Kong based company indicates that it has concluded an advance pricing agreement with the tax authorities. Two respondents are currently negotiating with the local tax authority for an advance pricing agreement. Eight respondents will consider negotiating an advance pricing agreement in the future. Twenty-one respondents indicate that they have no plans to apply for advance pricing agreements. Eleven respondents have not considered the issue at all.

Actual Case. For the purposes of this book a company was contacted in China to discuss the issue of transfer pricing as an illustration of the foregoing data. The Sino-Korean Limited Company is a recently established Equity Joint Venture enterprise. With a paid-in capital of RMB 1.8 billion, this company designs, develops, manufactures, and sells motor cars, including engines and many component parts, and has a registered company life of 30 years. The Korean parent company contributed 50% of the shares. There are well over 2,000 employees in

Table 10.11 Home country of the subsidiary respondent firms that are currently using or considering advance pricing agreements (APA)

Home country	Have concluded an APA with the local tax authority	Are currently negotiating with the local tax authority for an APA	Plan to apply for an APA with the local tax authority	Have no plans to apply for an APA with the local tax authority	Uncertain	Total
Hong Kong	1	0	1	6	2	10
Japan	0	0	2	1	1	4
Taiwan	0	1	1	2	1	5
USA	0	0	3	3	2	8
Others	0	1	1	9	5	16
Total	1	2	8	21	11	43

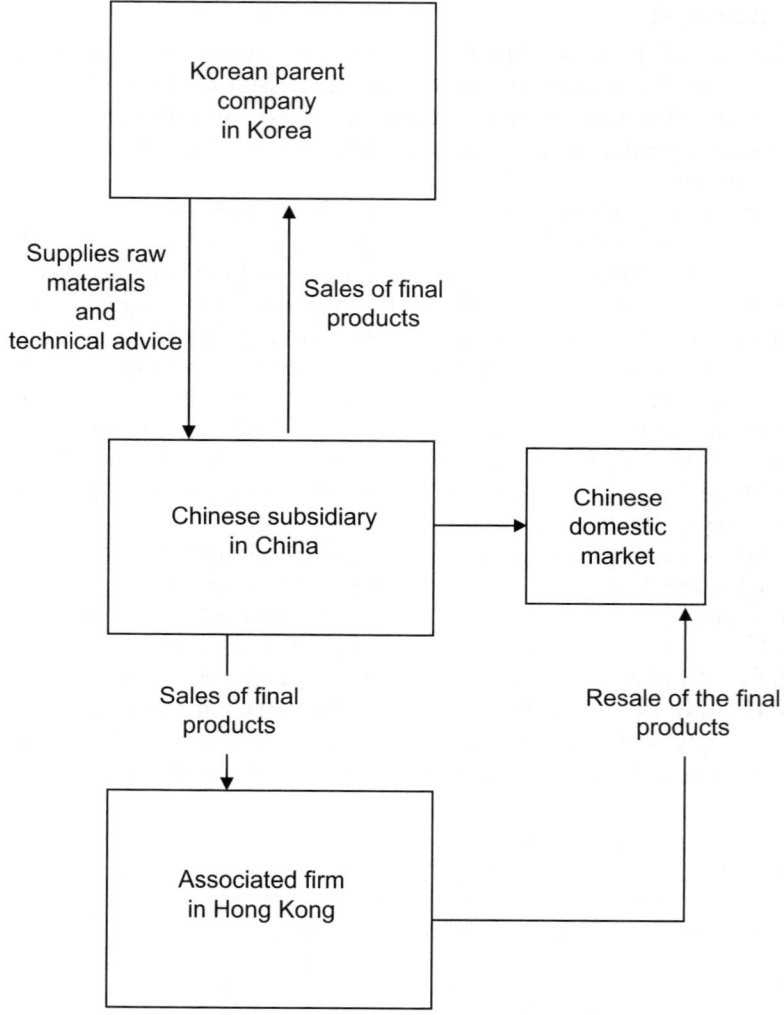

Figure 10.1 Transaction flows for a motor car company

this company. The Korean parent company provides raw materials, major components, and key production techniques to the Equity Joint Venture. The parent company established a separate department of the Chinese subsidiary with which it deals direct, over the head of the subsidiary's management, for the supply of raw materials. It is also responsible for the exports of the Chinese company's output. In return, the company pays management fees and royalties to its parent company according to its sales income.

As shown in Figure 10.1, the Chinese subsidiary receives its raw materials and technical assistance from its parent Korean company to which it sells part of its output. It sells another part of its output to its Hong Kong associated company which in turn sells this output back to the Chinese market. The subsidiary also sells the final part of its output direct into the Chinese market on its own account.

Transfer pricing in the company generally is conducted between the parent company and both the Chinese subsidiary and the Hong Kong subsidiary on the basis of negotiations by the general managers, but the parent company ultimately controls product pricing. The strategic consideration governing decisions on transfer pricing is to increase the company's market share. Until 2003, the company had not attracted the attentions of the tax authorities and had not been subject to an audit. The company uses the resale price method to regulate prices charged by the subsidiary to both the parent company and the Hong Kong subsidiary. The Chinese subsidiary was ignorant of the existence of advance pricing agreements, and therefore had never taken them into consideration. Staff members interviewed were ambiguous about the likelihood of being subject to future audits.

Summary

This chapter provides data illustrative of the perspectives, methods, priorities, and experiences regarding transfer pricing that characterize companies operating in China, as gathered by research for this book. Of particular note in this chapter is the importance of Hong Kong. This will be further enhanced as a result of the comprehensive arrangement concluded on 21 August 2006 between the Chinese Central Government and the Hong Kong Special Administrative Region Government for the avoidance of double taxation, the reduction of withholding taxes on dividends to 5–10% and of taxes on interests and royalties to 7% for Hong Kong investors in Mainland China and Hong Kong respectively, with effect from 1 January and 1 April 2007.

11
Audit in Action

Introduction

In common with other major trading countries, China prefers to see the use of the arm's length pricing principle applied in all transactions between foreign companies and their associated companies operating in China. In view of the widespread failure of companies to observe this principle in practice, however, China has adopted increasingly stringent measures to enforce the use of it, including the enactment of elaborate rules for the guidance of both the companies themselves and the tax authority staff who work to ensure compliance.

Cases of transfer pricing audits

To enhance an understanding of the transfer pricing audit practices in China, 16 audit cases were collected, variously subject to our translation. Five of these were operational cases obtained direct from the tax authorities, eight were training examples obtained direct from the tax authorities, and three were obtained from Chinese secondary sources. The detailed content and analysis of each of these cases are presented as follows.

Tangible goods

Audit Case 1: A Sino-Sweden Equity Joint Venture audited in 2000
- Background of the case

The Sino-Swedish Limited Company is an Equity Joint Venture established in 1992. With a paid-in capital of US$ 20.90 million, this company manufactures and sells telecommunication equipment and has a registered company life of 30 years. The Swedish parent company contributed 52% of the shares. There are about 600 employees in the company. The Swedish parent company provides raw materials, major components, and key production techniques to the Equity Joint Venture. It is also responsible for the exports of the Chinese company's output. In return, the company pays management fees and royalties to the parent company according to its sales income.

- Issues detected

Fluctuating profit patterns, with frequent interchanging of profits and losses. In 2000, the company paid management fees of RNB 389.39 million to its parent company. The tax authority considered this an unreasonable level of fees to pay to the parent company for the assets transferred.

- Selection of the method and adjustments

Using the comparable profit method, the tax authority adjusted the company's sales margin by 2%. This resulted in an increase of taxable revenue by RNB 1143.65 million and a corresponding corporate income tax charge of RNB 22.87 million.

Audit Case 2: A Hong Kong Wholly Owned Subsidiary audited in 2003
- Background of the case

This Hong Kong Wholly Owned Company was established in 1991. With a paid-in capital of RNB 2.8 million, the company manufactures and sells plastic toys, registered for a production period of 30 years. The Hong Kong parent company owns 100% of the shares. In return, the subsidiary sells all its goods to the parent company, which in turn sells them to the United States and European Countries.

- Issues detected

The company progressively expanded its scale of operations. But once the expiration of its legitimate tax holiday period arrived, its sales revenues continuously dropped. Its gross profit margin, with an average of 10.1%, was lower than that of enterprises in the same industry.

- Selection of the method and adjustments

Using the resale price method, the tax authority adjusted its profit margin to 15%. This resulted in an increase of taxable revenue of RNB 15.32 million and a corresponding corporate income tax charge of RNB 1.36 million.

Audit Case 3: A Hong Kong Wholly Owned Subsidiary audited in 1996
- Background of the case

This Hong Kong Wholly Owned Company was established in 1991. With a paid-in capital of US$ 1.6 million, it manufactures and sells sports shoes, with a registered production life of 50 years. Both the imports of its raw materials and the exports of its products are via its Hong Kong parent company.
- Issues detected

Its reported profit rate varied between plus and minus 1%, but its annual exports increased by 50%. The company continuously expanded its scale of operations. But once the expiration date of its tax holiday period arrived, its reported sales revenues continuously dropped.
- Selection of the method and adjustments

The tax authority considered that its sales price was lower than the market price. Using the comparable uncontrolled price method, the tax authority adjusted the company's profit margin to 15%. This resulted in an increased charge of corporate income tax of RNB 2.61 million.

Audit Case 4: A Sino-Hong Kong Wholly Owned Subsidiary audited in 1998
- Background of the case

The Sino-Hong Kong Wholly Owned Subsidiary was established in 1992. With a paid-in capital of US$ 19 million, this company manufactures and sells photocopiers, with a projected production life of 30 years. The parent company supplies all the raw materials and distributes all the product output to foreign markets.
- Issues detected

Production and sales decisions are determined by the Hong Kong company. In good market and production conditions, sales volumes between 1992 and 1997 constantly increased, but at the same time the costs of production rose considerably, the costs of raw material in particular claiming a higher percentage of total costs. As a result the sales profit margin shrank.
- Selection of the method and adjustments

Obtaining comparable data from various sources, the tax authority used the resale price method to adjust the company's gross profit margin from 7% to 11%, resulting in an assessed additional taxable income of RNB 98.93 million, with a liability to pay RNB 11.87 million.

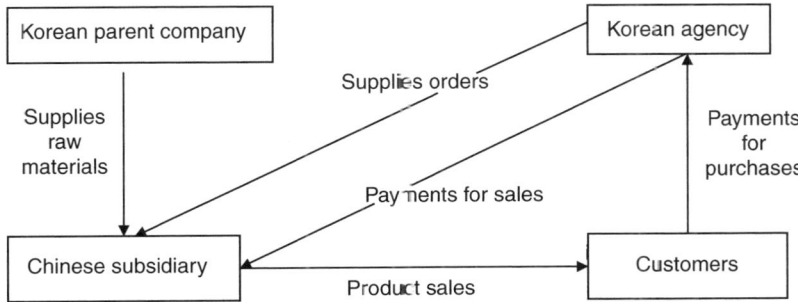

Figure 11.1 Transaction flows for Audit Case 5

Audit Case 5: A Sino-Korean Wholly Owned Subsidiary audited in 2000
- Background of the case

The Sino-Korean Wholly Owned Subsidiary was established in 1993. This company has a projected production life of 30 years, manufacturing and selling a variety of footwear products. The parent company supplies all the raw materials and authorizes its subsidiary to supply customers direct, the orders for which are transmitted to the subsidiary by an agency in Korea which is independent of the parent company. Customers pay this agency direct for their purchases and the agency then reimburses the subsidiary, as shown in Figure 11.1.

- Issues detected

The subsidiary's sales steadily increased and its gross profit margin remained at 9% for several years, with a sales profit rate of minus 3%, but suddenly, in 1999, these performance indicators respectively dropped to 0.33% and minus 7.47%. Its gross profit margins for the years 1997 to 1999 were respectively 5.9%, 8.04%, and 0.33%. These fluctuations attracted the interest of the tax authority and led to an audit.

- Selection of the method and adjustments

The tax authority was unable to obtain information from the parent company and its Korean agency, so it used the cost plus method to adjust the subsidiary's prices. It found that the normal sales gross profit margins for the industry at large were between 7% and 10%. The subsidiary's sales gross profit margin was adjusted to 8%, resulting in an additional tax payment of RNB 12 million.

Audit Case 6: A Sino-Japanese Wholly Owned Subsidiary audited in 2000
- Background of the case

The Sino-Japanese Wholly Owned Subsidiary was established in 1993. This clothing company manufactures and sells uniforms. The parent company supplies all the raw materials and identifies the customers but authorizes the subsidiary to conduct business direct with the customers.
- Issues detected

The company moved into profit in 1995 after its second year of operation but in 1997 and 1998 it reported losses, followed by a small profit in 1999. Its gross profit margins for the years 1994 to 1999 were respectively 11.66%, 15.39%, 17.58%, 8.06%, 28.22%, and 18.79%.
- Selection of the method and adjustments

The tax authority deemed the company's overall gross profit margin to be 15% per year, except for 1997 when it was deemed to be 12% in a year of difficult trading conditions. Using the comparable profit method, the tax authority adjusted the company's additional taxable income to RNB 943,740.97, giving rise to an extra tax charge of RNB 42,549.45.

Audit Case 7: A Sino-American Cooperative Joint Venture audited in 2000
- Background of the case

The Sino-American Cooperative Joint Venture was established in 1989. With a paid-in capital of US$ 1.8 million, this company manufactures and sells footwear with a projected production life of 15 years. The Chinese company took up 39% of the foundation capital, the American company taking up 61%. The American company supplies all the raw materials and distributes all the product output.
- Issues detected

Production and sales decisions are determined by the American company. During the period 1990 to 1994 the company posted a profit but since then reported continuous but increasing losses, allegedly caused by the increasing prices of the company's imported raw materials from the American associated company. After 1999 the company reported moving into profit again.
- Selection of the method and adjustments

The company's products were manifestly of a superior quality compared with similar products from domestic companies, so the tax authorities were unable to use the comparable uncontrolled price method when they decided to audit the company. They chose instead to apply the cost plus method to adjust the profits of the company. The taxable income was adjusted to RNB 1,128,070.

Audit Case 8: A Sino-Korean Cooperative Joint Venture audited in 2000
- Background of the case

A Sino-Korean Equity Joint Venture was established in 1993. With a paid-in capital of US$ 1.2 million, this company manufactures and sells footwear with a projected production life of 20 years. Raw materials for its production are imported from its parent company in Korea. All its products are exported to foreign customers at the direction and under the control of the parent company, and at prices determined by it.

- Issues detected

Sales revenues from 1997 to 1999 were respectively reported as RNB 302,087,000, RNB 437,682,000, and RNB 534,883,000. At the same time the company's gross profit margin rates were shown as 10.67%, 9.08%, and 7.31%. The tax authority took note of this apparent anomaly and subjected the company to an audit, suspecting that the prices paid by the company for imported materials were too high and those received for its finished products were too low.

- Selection of the method and adjustments

The tax authority was unable to obtain the selling prices of the company's products in its overseas markets. Therefore, it was unable to use the comparable uncontrolled price method in deciding to audit the company. Instead, the cost plus method was applied to adjust the profits of the company and establish that the normal gross profit margin range for the industry at large was 7% to 10%. But because the company's products were marketed under a famous brand name they determined that the gross profit margin should be higher than the average, pegging it at 15%. This resulted in an increase of taxable revenue by RNB 9,039,520 and a corresponding corporate income tax charge of RNB 1,084,740.

Audit Case 9: A Sino-Japanese Equity Joint Venture audited in 2000
- Background of the case

A Sino-Japanese Equity Joint Venture was established in 1995. With a paid-in capital of US$ 0.6 million, this company manufactures and sells foodstuffs. Ninety per cent of its products are exported to other associated companies in Japan. From 1996 to 1999 the yearly total transactions with these related companies were respectively RNB 7.94 million, RNB 5.57 million, RNB 3.03 million, and RNB 8.42 million.

- Issues detected

The tax authority found that the company's posted gross profit margins and sales volumes fluctuated. In 1996 and 1997 its gross profit margins were lower than in other years whilst the unit costs of production increased by 20%, yet its sales prices remained lower than in other years. In addition, the tax authority determined that export prices were wholly fixed by the Japanese parent company, concluding that for the two years 1996 and 1997, the company had engaged in transfer pricing manipulations, thereby justifying an audit.

- Selection of the method and adjustments

The tax authority calculated that the gross profit margin should be 16.08% on the basis of the sales revenues and the cost of sales during the period 1996 to 1999. It adjusted the taxable profit of the company to RNB 371,635.36, a figure which they arrived at by using the comparable profit method.

Audit Case 10: A Sino-Japanese Equity Joint Venture audited in 1999.

- Background of the case

A Sino-Japan Equity Joint Venture was established in 1992. This company manufactures and sells electric generators. Raw materials and component parts are imported from the parent company in Japan, which also purchases all the output for distribution in the Japanese market.

- Issues detected

The tax authority found that the company's sales revenues increased while its financial and administrative expenses remained static. The expenses for sales decreased. The sales profit rate remained negative at minus 2%. The tax authority also found that the cost of sales was shown as 92% of sales revenues. Since the main part of the total cost of sales was the raw materials as imported from Japan, they suspected that the prices paid for them were too high. In addition, it was found that the parent company had made fresh capital injections into their subsidiary, although it was showing repeated losses. Taken together, these considerations prompted an audit.

- Selection of the method and adjustments

It was discovered that the expenses incurred by this company were significantly in excess of the average levels for the industry at large. At the same time its sales profit rates were lower than those for companies in the same industry. For the years 1997, 1998, and 1999, the parent company's resale profit margins were found to be 21.09%, 20.44%, and 25.43% respectively. These were judged to be too high. The tax authorities consequently adjusted the sales profit rates of the company to be 4%, 4.5%, and 5%. Based on this outcome, the taxable profit of the company was adjusted to RNB 3,177,453.43, a figure which they arrived at by using the comparable profit method, giving rise to additional tax charges.

Audit Case 11: A Sino-Hong Kong Equity Joint Venture audited in 1995
- Background of the case

A Sino-Hong Kong Equity Joint Venture was established in 1988. This company manufactures and sells telecommunication equipment. Raw materials and component parts are imported from the parent company in Hong Kong, which also purchases all the output and is responsible for the sale of it. The Hong Kong partner holds 60% of the shares of the company.
- Issues detected

The tax authorities found that the imported raw materials from Hong Kong were being charged at 30% over the normal market price. In contrast, the sales prices of the finished goods charged to the Hong Kong partner were lower by 20% than normal market prices.
- Selection of the method and adjustments

The tax authorities used the comparable uncontrolled price method to adjust the costs of imported raw materials and the prices of exported finished goods. As a consequence, the profits of the company were shown as having increased from minus US$ 0.52 million to US$ 4.02 million, thereby increasing the tax revenues accruing to the government.

Audit Case 12: A Sino-Japanese Wholly Owned Subsidiary, audited in 1999.
- Background of the case

This company was established in 1995 as an Equity Joint Venture, with a paid-in capital of US$ 170,000 to manufacture and sell cartoon films, with a projected production life of 11 years, but in 1996 the company was put on a new footing as a wholly owned company.
- Issues detected

The company reported yearly losses from the start to 1998, losses being posted as RNB 500,000 for 1995, RNB 66,000 for 1996, RNB 223,000 for 1997, and RNB 218,000 for 1998, totaling well over RNB 1 million. Over these years its annual profit rate was minus 24.1%, whereas the average annual profit rate for the industry at large was 10%. The prices paid for raw materials and for product outputs were controlled by the parent company. Both the raw materials involved and the output itself are channeled through the parent company, the former being obtained from international markets and the latter being sold internationally.

- Selection of the method and adjustments

The tax authority was unable to obtain the prices ultimately charged by the parent company. It was therefore unable to apply the resale price method, but was obliged to use the comparable uncontrolled price method to adjust the company's tax liability when it subjected the company to an audit. It compared this company's reported figures with those of a Taiwanese company with a similar product. The company's combined taxable income for the years 1996 and 1997 was adjusted to RNB 3,449,343.7, with a consequent tax payment of RNB 70,649.21.

Audit Case 13: A Sino-United Kingdom Wholly Owned Subsidiary, audited in 1999.
- Background of the case

This company was established in 1993 as a Wholly Owned Subsidiary by a Hong Kong company, with a paid-in capital of US$ 1 million to manufacture and sell office equipment. The Hong Kong company was in turn a subsidiary of its parent company in the United Kingdom.
- Issues detected

The subsidiary imports its raw materials from the Hong Kong company through an agent appointed by the latter, and sells its products direct into the Chinese market. The tax authority found that the prices which had to be paid by the subsidiary for its raw materials to the agent were greatly in excess of the prices which the Hong Kong company charged the agent, to the extent of 28.3%. For the years 1996 to 1998 it was found that the Kong Kong company accumulated profits amounting to HK$ 62,065,228, with an average profit rate of 10.89%, while the Chinese subsidiary made a total loss for the two years of RNB 1,223,005.68, with an average posted profit rate of minus 0.22%.
- Selection of the method and adjustments

The tax authority was unable to obtain the price information from the Hong Kong company but ascertained that the average profit rate for the same industry at large was 5%. Using the comparable profit method the tax authority adjusted the total taxable income of the company for the years 1996 to 1998 to RNB 28,200,768.3, with a consequent tax payment of RNB 6,768,184.63.

Intangible goods

Audit Case 14: A Japanese Wholly Owned Subsidiary audited in 2003
- Background of the case

The Japanese Wholly Owned Company was established in 1991. With a paid-in capital of Yen 2 billion, this company manufactures and sells

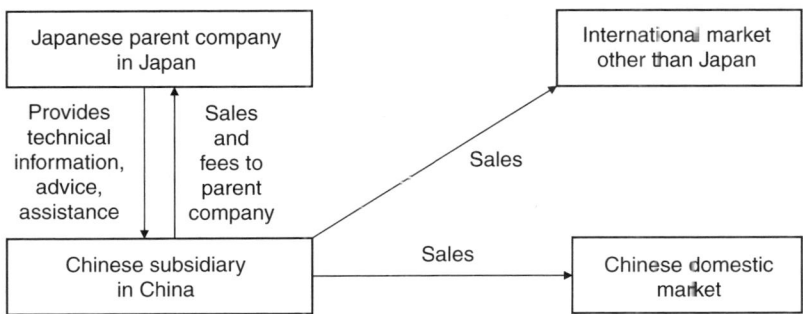

Figure 11.2 Transaction flows for Audit Case 14

precision medical instruments such as thermometers and sphygmomanometers, with a registered production life of 50 years. Eighty-five per cent of its products are exported to the overseas market through its Japanese parent company, as shown in Figure 11.2.

- Issues detected

Production and operational decisions were in the control of the parent company. The subsidiary was empowered to sell its products direct to the Chinese domestic market and also to export to foreign markets with the exception of Japan, but was in addition required to supply products to the parent company for the Japanese market. The Japanese parent company provided technical information, advice and assistance. Product prices charged to the parent company were 10% less than those charged to customers in the Chinese domestic market and to overseas markets other than Japan. The purpose of this differential was to amass extra income to enable the subsidiary at a later date to make payments to the parent company, ostensibly by way of management and royalty fees, for the intangible assets which it provided. Behind this purpose, in the view of the tax authority, was the objective of avoiding the withholding tax to which these payments would have been liable.

- Selection of the method and adjustments

The prices that the subsidiary charged the parent company were 10% lower than those charged in the domestic and foreign markets other than Japan. The subsidiary did not pay the management fees and royalty fees that would normally be due to its parent company, amounting to the equivalent of 10% of the company's revenues from these sales. By not paying these fees, the tax authority discovered that each year during the period 1993 to 1999, the company had failed to pay the required withholding tax to the Chinese tax authority. Using the comparable uncontrolled price method, the tax authority adjusted the management fees and royalty fees due during 1993 and 1998 to RMB 266.68 million. It required the subsidiary to pay this to the parent company and was duly taxed on it. This resulted in an increase of withholding tax of RMB 26.66 million. In 1999, the additional payments of management fees and royalty fees were fixed at RMB 77.6 million. This resulted in an increased withholding tax of RMB 7.76 million.

Services

Audit Case 15: A Sino-Hong Kong Equity Joint Venture audited in 1996
- Background of the case

A Sino-Hong Kong Equity Joint Venture was established in 1991. Its registered capital is RNB 12 million. The Chinese part of the venture contributed RNB 7.2 million, as an investment, the Hong Kong element contributing the balance of the capital and undertaking to manage the practical activities necessary to operate the company's business, which consists of operating a high quality cruise ship.
- Issues detected

The tax authorities found that the Hong Kong partner was responsible for the world wide marketing of the ship's cruise programme and received payments from the passengers who applied to travel on it. However, the portion of these revenues passed over to the joint venture company were incommensurate with what was due to it.
- Selection of the method and adjustments

The tax authorities used the comparable uncontrolled price method to correct this anomaly when they subjected the company to an audit. The Hong Kong partner was obliged to pay the Joint Venture Company RNB 2,275,280.12, and was charged with an additional tax payment and a penalty amounting in total to RNB 1,340,787.86.

Finance

Audit Case 16: A Sino-Hong Kong Equity Joint Venture audited in 1998
- Background of the case

A Sino-Hong Kong Equity Joint Venture was established in 1995. Its registered capital is US$ 20 million. Its production and operations are wholly controlled by its parent company in Hong Kong.
- Issues detected

The tax authorities found that in 1998 the company was in receipt of loans from the parent company to a total of RNB 34.3 million, on which it paid loan interest amounting to RNB 4.81 million. In addition, in 1998, the parent supplied working capital loans of RNB 40.16 million in seven instalments. The interest rates on these seven instalments varied at the following rates: 10.15%, 9.85%, and 8.9%. The loan rate for China's Central Bank at the same time was 8.64%. The tax authority suspected that the company's profits were being transferred to the parent company by way of these perceived high loan interest rates.

- Selection of the method and adjustments

The tax authority took the Bank of China loan capital rates as the benchmark, calculating thereby that the company had overpaid interest rates to a total of RNB 627,438.42. As a result, the company was obliged to make an interim tax payment of RNB 94,115.76.

Summary

Table 11.1 summarizes the specific characteristics of the 16 audit cases. Among them the following may be noted:

1. Six companies are owned by Hong Kong parent firms, five by Japanese firms, two by Korean firms, one by a United Kingdom firm, one by a Swedish firm, and one by a United States firm.
2. Fourteen companies are in manufacturing industries, one in a service industry, and one in a business of an undisclosed nature.
3. Seven companies are wholly foreign owned, seven companies are equity joint venture, and two companies are cooperative joint venture.
4. Fourteen companies were investigated for their imports and exports, one company was investigated for intercompany transfers of intangible goods, one company was investigated for intercompany transfers of services, and one company was investigated for intercompany loans and interest payments.
5. Six companies were audited and suffered income adjustments by the comparable uncontrolled price method, five companies by the comparable profit method, three companies by the cost plus method, and two companies by the resale price method.

Table 11.1 Summary of audit cases

Case	Home country	Industry	Legal Form	Transactions Investigated	Grounds for Audit	Income Reallocation Method Used
1	Sweden	Telecommunication equipment	Equity joint venture	Raw materials imported, sales discounts, and fees for services	Fluctuating profit patterns, with frequent interchanging of profits and losses. Unreasonable expenses paid to associated enterprises.	Comparable profits
2	Hong Kong	Plastic toys	Wholly foreign owned	Goods exported	A sudden and significant drop in profits after the expiration of a preferential tax treatment period. Lower profits or losses for an extended period, but a continuously expanding scale of operations.	Resale price
3	Hong Kong	Sports shoes	Wholly foreign owned	Raw materials imported. Goods exported	Lower profits or losses for an extended period, but a continuously expanding scale of operations.	Comparable uncontrolled price
4	Hong Kong	Photocopiers	Wholly foreign owned	Raw materials imported. Goods exported	Production and sales decisions determined by the parent company. Lower profitability than enterprises in the same industry. Unreasonable expenses paid to associated enterprises	Resale price

Table 11.1 Summary of audit cases – continued

Case	Home country	Industry	Legal Form	Transactions Investigated	Grounds for Audit	Income Reallocation Method Used
5	Korea	Footwear	Wholly foreign owned	Raw materials imported. Goods exported	Fluctuating profit patterns, with frequent interchanging of profits and losses.	Cost plus
6	Japan	Uniforms	Equity joint venture	Raw materials imported. Goods exported	Production and operational decisions controlled by associated enterprises. Large transaction amounts with associated enterprises. Long periods of losses.	Comparable profits
7	United States	Footwear	Cooperative joint venture	Raw materials imported. Goods exported	Production and operational decisions controlled by associated enterprises. Fluctuating profit patterns, with frequent interchanging of profits and losses.	Cost plus
8	Korea	Footwear	Cooperative Joint Venture	Raw materials imported. Goods exported	Unreasonable expenses paid to associated enterprises.	Cost plus
9	Japan	Foodstuffs	Equity joint venture	Raw materials imported. Goods exported	Fluctuating profit patterns, with frequent interchanging of profits and losses.	Comparable profits
10	Japan	Electric generators	Equity joint venture	Raw materials imported.	Lower profits or losses for an extended period, but	Comparable profits

Table 11.1 Summary of audit cases – *continued*

Case	Home country	Industry	Legal Form	Transactions Investigated	Grounds for Audit	Income Reallocation Method Used
11	Hong Kong	Telecommunication equipment	Equity joint venture	Goods exported	a continuously expanding scale of operations. Lower average profitability than enterprises in the same industry	Comparable uncontrolled price
12	Japan	Cartoon films	Wholly foreign owned	Raw materials imported. Goods exported	Unreasonable expenses paid to associated enterprises	Comparable uncontrolled price
13	Hong Kong	Office equipment	Wholly foreign owned	Raw materials imported. Goods exported	Production and sales decisions determined by the parent company. Long periods of losses.	Comparable profits
14	Japan	Precision medical instruments	Wholly foreign owned	Raw materials imported. Goods exported	Unreasonable expenses paid to associated enterprises	Comparable uncontrolled price
15	Hong Kong	Travel services	Equity joint venture	Goods exported. Management fees	Production and operational decisions controlled by associated enterprises. Avoidance of paying withholding taxes	Comparable uncontrolled price
15	Hong Kong	Travel services	Equity joint venture	Services	Paying excessive fees for services provided by associated enterprises,	Comparable uncontrolled price
16	Hong Kong	Unknown	Equity joint venture	Loans and interest payments	Borrowing funds from its controlling firm and paying excessive interest rates on the loans	Comparable uncontrolled price

12
Audit Risk Levels

Introduction

Tax avoidance and evasion are widely practised in China in every taxation category but none more so than in the field of transfer pricing. Within the last five years it has been estimated that about 80% of foreign investment enterprises have been guilty of tax evasion. In 1997 the number of businesses registered was 24 times greater than the number of registrations of taxpayers, a differential that within two years increased to 303 times (Mo, 2003, pp. 80–4).

Personal perspectives of tax officials

For the purposes of this book, consultation with four tax authorities presiding over contrasting industrial and social areas in China revealed their deep concern that, by means of transfer pricing practices, foreign investment enterprises are not actually meeting their legal obligations and paying their fair share of taxes in China. They all justify their concern by citing the serious extent of the shortfall of revenues from taxation as an inhibiting factor for the development of the country. Their *ad hoc* comments, illustrating and explaining their concern, include the following, verbatim, subject to translation.

'We have noted that many foreign investment enterprises report persistent losses but continue to expand their operations. Except for normal operating losses, a number of foreign investment enterprises may engage in tax avoidance by transferring their profits abroad and reporting losses in China.'

'Foreign investment enterprises highly rely on imported inputs including machinery and equipment, intermediate products and raw materials. Many foreign investment enterprises have reported operating losses. Some of those foreign investment enterprises may be losses engineered by the importing of materials and equipment into China from their overseas associates at a high price and the exporting of goods to their affiliated firms abroad at a low price. The issue of tax avoidance by transfer pricing is becoming all the more pressing as the number and types of cross-border transactions are expected to increase as the volume of multinational enterprises doing business in China continues to grow.'

In some parts of China transfer pricing manipulations are not a significant practical concern for the tax authority. The officers of an inland city tax authority explained the reasons for their relative lack of attention to transfer pricing issues as follows.

'Compared with the coastal cities in China, transfer pricing manipulation is not a serious concern to our tax authority. In the city, corporate income tax accounts for a relatively small proportion of total tax revenue. On average, corporate income taxes contributed only 16.7% of the total tax revenue in 2002. As an inland city, it is not easy for us to attract foreign direct investments. The local government often attempts to provide an attractive investment environment for foreign investors and therefore is reluctant for the tax authority to adopt a strict transfer pricing scrutiny for fear of inducing a flight of capital. In addition, from the government's viewpoint, the losses of corporate income taxes collected from foreign investment enterprises can be more than compensated for by a significant increase in foreign direct investment, as the increased foreign investment should produce significant increases in revenues from other more productive taxes such as value-added taxes, consumption taxes, and business taxes. Another reason is that most of the foreign investment enterprises operating in the city are newly established and should still be covered by tax holiday and tax rate reduction concessions. Income adjustments to related party transactions of these foreign investment enterprises do not significantly affect the collection of tax revenues. Later on, the issue for us will become more pressing with the completion of tax holidays.'

Although the inland city tax authority has not devoted much attention to transfer pricing issues in the past, it is now preparing to challenge foreign investment enterprises on the issue of transfer pricing.

'Though the auditing department was established in 1992, the government worries that the imposition of tight control practices might deter foreign investment in the city. For many years, our central objective was to attract foreign investments rather than to collect income tax revenues from foreign investment enterprises. Not until very recent years has our tax authority noted the transfer pricing manipulation issue and taken steps to combat tax avoidance, via transfer pricing abuses, by foreign investment enterprises in the city. At present, there are four tax officers who fully concentrate on transfer pricing tax auditing in our tax authority.'

In the case of China, to shift profits made by a Chinese subsidiary to the home country of its parent company, the parent company can use transfer pricing manipulation in a simple form, such as deliberately overpricing imports sent from the parent company to its Chinese subsidiary, or intentionally undervaluing exports by the subsidiary to its parent firm. An interviewed tax officer describes the situation. 'It is often the case that an overseas parent company controls the purchases and sales of products of a foreign investment enterprise that operates in China. On the one hand, it intentionally inflates the price of equipment, raw materials and spare parts purchased and imported by the Chinese subsidiary. On the other hand, it suppresses the prices of finished products exported from China.'

Tax authority perspectives

The Chinese transfer pricing rules specify the company features by which high-risk foreign investment enterprises can be identified. They mandate the Chinese tax authorities to audit at least 30% of the enterprises on the target list of companies that have been identified by these means. These company features include the following:

1. Production and operational decisions controlled by associated enterprises
2. Large transaction amounts with associated enterprises
3. Long periods of losses – for more than two consecutive years
4. Lower profits or losses for an extended period, but continuously expanding scale of operations
5. Fluctuating profit patterns, with frequent interchanging of profits and losses
6. Transactions with associated enterprises established in tax havens
7. Lower profitability than enterprises in the same industry
8. Lower profit margins than other group companies
9. Unreasonable expenses paid to associated enterprises
10. Sudden, significant drop in profits after a preferential tax treatment period.

Following discussions with tax officials for the purposes of this book, a questionnaire based upon them was sent to 80 Chinese tax authorities to discover the levels of concern they had about transfer pricing abuses according to each of the above listed ten types of ownership-production-sales-financial profiles displayed between foreign investment enterprises and their associate companies operating in China. They were invited to express this by weighting each of the ten features according to its perceived importance for concealing transfer pricing abuses.

The underlying assumption entertained was that tax officers intensify their scrutiny of those firms they suspect of transfer pricing manipulations. Thirty-eight returns were obtained. The results from these respondent tax authorities are presented in Table 12.1, in descending order of importance.

It can be seen that 'production and operational decisions controlled by associated enterprises' is indicated by the respondents as being the most significant factor for generating transfer pricing abuses. Other significant factors include 'lower profits or losses for an extended

Table 12.1 Company features most likely to encourage transfer pricing abuses as cited by tax authorities

Company Features	Means	SD
Production and operational decisions controlled by associated enterprises	4.68	0.525
Lower profits or losses for an extended period, but continuously expanding scale of operations	4.53	0.603
Sudden, significant drop in profits after a preferential tax treatment period	4.42	0.683
Transactions with associated enterprises established in tax havens	4.34	0.815
Lower profitability than enterprises in the same industry	4.34	2.507
Large transaction amounts with associated enterprises	4.32	0.525
Unreasonable expenses paid to associated enterprises	4.16	0.973
Long periods of losses – for more than two consecutive years	4.08	0.673
Fluctuating profit patterns, with frequent interchanging of profits and losses	3.97	0.716
Lower profit margins than other group companies	3.79	0.741

Table 12.2 Methods used by tax authorities to calculate true liabilities and tax payment adjustments in cases of transfer pricing abuse

Method	Number of tax authorities	Percentage
Comparable profit	36	31.6**
Cost plus	32	28.1
Comparable uncontrolled price	23	20.2
Resale price	17	14.9
Profit split	5	4.4
Global formulary apportionment	1	0.9
Total	114*	100

Note: * 12 tax authorities used more than one transfer pricing method.
**rounded

period, but continuously expanding scale of operations', 'sudden, significant drop in profits after a preferential tax treatment period', 'transactions with associated enterprises established in tax havens', and 'lower profitability than enterprises in the same industry'.

Three features are indicated as being of relatively greater concern by the respondent tax authorities. They are 'large transaction amounts with associated enterprises', 'unreasonable expenses paid to associated enterprises', and 'long periods of losses – for more than two consecutive years'. Variables that are of moderate concern include 'fluctuating profit patterns, with frequent interchanging of profits and losses', and 'lower profit margins than other group companies'.

The Chinese tax authorities were also asked to state the methods they used for calculating a company's true liabilities and for adjusting its payments of taxes when it had been found guilty of transfer pricing manipulations with its related companies. The methods as reported by the 38 respondent tax authorities are shown in Table 12.2.

It can be seen that the method most commonly used is 'comparable profit', as adopted by 36 (31.6%) tax authorities in the sample. Other popular methods used are 'cost plus', 'comparable uncontrolled price', and 'resale price', respectively by 32 (28.1%), 23 (20.2%), and 17 (14.9%) of the tax authorities. The least widely used methods in the sample include 'profit split' and 'global formulary apportionment'.

Audit risk model

Whilst the interests of the tax authorities in China are focused on collecting the maximum possible revenues arising from the full legitimate liabilities of a foreign investment enterprise, in practice these of necessity are constrained by the practicalities and capabilities of the staff available for the purpose. In practice therefore there has been plenty of scope for tax evasion and avoidance by way of transfer pricing practices.

Towards a more equitable taxation system overall, and as an encouragement of more conformity to its tax laws, China intends to establish a common rate of company taxation for both domestic and foreign investment enterprises. But since this expected level of taxation is in the region of 25%, there will be persistent and strong incentives for companies to consider transfer pricing solutions to achieve reductions in tax liabilities – in light of the fact that 25% represents about double the rate that has applied in the past, which itself has always been enough to encourage companies to indulge transfer pricing manoeuvres for the purpose of tax evasion and avoidance.

Coupled with this expected development is the likelihood of the diminution or abolition of previously widespread tax concessions of various kinds, especially in manufacturing fields. In view of the endemic custom of tax evasion and avoidance in China, it may be predicted with a degree of confidence that the propensity for companies to use transfer pricing to minimize their tax liabilities will continue to exist and may actually increase from existing levels. Correspondingly, a more sophisticated and effective defensive system will be developed by the tax authorities to combat the practice, the main instrument of which will be a more widespread and competent audit system.

The experience of China's tax authorities in dealing with foreign investment enterprises which use transfer pricing to escape their fiscal liabilities has been long enough to provide evidence of the range of variables which are subject to their scrutiny and which govern their decision to subject a company to an audit.

These variables fall into two main categories – those which involve *conditional factors* and those which involve *volitional factors*.

Conditional factors. These are the size of the company, its country of origin, the level of foreign ownership in terms of control over company decisions and operations, and the company's previous relationship record with the tax authorities.

Audit Probability Level	Lower Risk	Higher Risk
Size	Larger Companies	Medium/Smaller Companies

Country of Origin	Most Home Countries	Hong Kong, Japan, Taiwan
Foreign Ownership	Local Autonomy	Complete External Control
Tax Authorities	Good Record	Bad Record

Volitional Factors. These include the many courses of action that are deliberately chosen, or unknowingly taken, or are allowed to occur by default, that breach fiscal laws and regulations. The nine factors listed below are in descending order of importance as indicated by the 38 tax authorities which were contacted for the purposes of this book.

Table 12.3 Company performance variables affecting audit risk levels

Low Audit Risk		High Audit Risk
Rising profits with company expansion	1	Protracted low profits/losses with company expansion
Rising profits after tax concessions end	2	Sudden significant fall in profit after tax concessions end
No transactions with associates in tax haven countries	3	Transactions with associates In tax haven countries
Comparable profitability levels for the industry at large	4	Profitability levels inconsistent with the industry at large
Moderate volume of transactions with foreign associates	5	Excessive volume of transactions with foreign associates
Reasonable expenses paid to foreign associates	6	Unusually large expenses paid to foreign associates
Losses posted for no more than two consecutive years	7	Losses posted for more than two consecutive years
Steady profit growth	8	Fluctuating profits and losses
Similar profit margins to those of associated companies	9	Lower profit margins than those of associated companies

Company track records. The performance of companies in practice across the range of volitional factors listed above and numbered 1–9 is inevitably varied but the variations may be depicted by classifying performances into four categories of risk takers.

*Category 1. **The Perfectionists.*** These are companies that from start to finish have every intention of abiding fully by the laws and regulations governing transfer pricing and tax liabilities. Their profile is describable in terms of all factors listed in the Low Audit Risk Category above. According to research data and Chinese official reports, The Perfectionists constitute a small minority of foreign investment enterprises operating in China, but this is the category that recent and promised improvements in the structure, technology, and methodologies by which the taxation system will be operated, are designed to enlarge.

Category 2. **The Incorrigibles.** These are the companies which from start to finish adopt a contemptuous attitude to their legal tax liabilities. They identify with the traditionally widespread tax evasion and avoidance practices of Chinese nationals. The risks involved and indeed any previous clashes with the tax authorities fail to deter them from a determined intention to exploit the opportunities to maximize company advantages by transfer pricing devices whenever and wherever they can be employed. The Incorrigibles constitute a substantial percentage of companies whose profile is describable in terms of all the High Audit Risk category items listed above. In representing the exact opposite of the Perfectionists, the Incorrigibles are becoming the main target of the improved audit system by which the authorities plan to enforce compliance with regard to fiscal liabilities.

Category 3. **The Repentants.** These are the companies whose aberrant behaviour has been corrected either as a result of a change of attitude within the company in the light of its interests in the Chinese environment, or as a result of an investigation and audit by the tax authorities. Where the latter is the determining reason for a change to probity, the tax authorities are able to conclude that their action has been effective in the direction intended. The Repentants may have indulged any number of the practices listed in the High Audit Risk column above but subsequently have veered to the corresponding practices listed in the Low Audit Risk column, thereby potentially shedding the attention of the tax authorities.

Category 4. **The Apostates.** These are the companies that first attempted to live fully up to their obligations under the tax laws and regulations but later perceived that lucrative returns were in the offing by means of the adroit practice of transfer pricing. Furthermore, they became aware of the extent of tax evasion and avoidance of others by these means, drawing a conclusion in terms of their own competitive disadvantage. The Apostates may have formerly observed any of the practices in the Low Audit Risk column above but subsequently veered to the corresponding practices listed in the High Audit Risk column, thereby potentially attracting the greater attention of the tax authorities.

Audit policy and practice development

In the past few years, hundreds of anti-tax avoidance officials have been trained and specific audit goals have been established. The tax authorities in China, from the state level down to local district level, are extending their tax collection efforts by employing transfer pricing audits. However, up to now, only a few anti-tax avoidance officials in the Chinese coastal city tax authorities have substantial investigative and auditing experience in the realm of transfer pricing. The majority of tax officials have limited knowledge and experience of transfer pricing issues. The tax officials interviewed were invited to suggest how the Chinese transfer pricing monitoring system could be improved. Their suggestions are summarized as follows.

Information Exchange with Foreign Tax Authorities. China has signed income tax treaties with more than eighty countries around the world. The State Administration of Taxation is responsible for exchanging information with the competent authorities of foreign tax treaty countries. An international network could be set up for the routine exchange of information with foreign tax authorities. Such a system would allow tax officials to access financial information from foreign companies.

Establishment of an Appropriate Transfer Pricing Computerized Information Administrative and Monitoring System. As the highest tax authority in China, the State Administration of Taxation should establish nationwide, transfer-pricing-related software to facilitate the collection of comparable information. To date, the State Administration of Taxation has installed transfer pricing related software. This national computer system could facilitate the ability of Chinese tax authorities at different levels to share transfer pricing information.

Improving the Technical Competence of Tax Officials. The Chinese tax authorities should provide training for tax officials in transfer pricing. Since 1991, China has been sending delegations from its tax authorities to The Netherlands, Japan, and the United States for training in transfer pricing. In addition, the State Administration of Taxation has organized several transfer pricing training seminars for tax officers from local tax authorities. Components of study include the OECD approach to transfer pricing, a functional and risk analysis, the identification of comparable transactions and comparable unrelated entities, and an evaluation of various transfer pricing methods. Transfer pricing specialist teams should be set up by all provincial level tax authorities. These transfer pricing specialist teams should then collaborate with other authorities in China to strengthen their transfer pricing audit capabilities.

On the improvement of the Chinese transfer pricing monitoring system, some comments from replies to an open question in the survey of the provincial and city tax authorities are quoted verbatim, subject to translation, as follows:

- 'Tax examiners are often frustrated in their attempts to gather evidence of transfer pricing abuses. The exchange of tax information with domestic and overseas counterparts would allow them to obtain the necessary information for combating international tax evasion and avoidance.'
- 'An international exchange network could be set up for routine information exchanges with foreign tax authorities. To strengthen the enforcement of transfer pricing regulations, tax authorities should enhance cooperation with other authorities such as customs, industrial and commercial departments.'
- 'We need to use computers more for data collection and financial analyses, and to establish internal databases to be available to the various levels of tax authorities by way of computer networks.'
- 'The government should strengthen and improve the transfer pricing laws and regulations.'
- 'Since no serious punishments are imposed for transfer pricing abuses, even when we succeed in challenging a related party transaction, it is normally worthwhile for a foreign investment enterprise to "try it on". To strengthen the enforcement of transfer pricing investigations, it is imperative to introduce specific transfer pricing penalties in the tax law. The current low penalty law must be changed to impose on violators real financial consequences if they fail to comply.'
- 'Inadequate information exchange systems with overseas counterparts make it difficult to obtain the sales prices of overseas associated companies.'
- 'We need to establish information systems providing the systematic collection and analysis of prices and profits for each industry involved at large.'
- 'At present the tax authorities can only impose an adjustment directly on the associated company operating in China. In the event of their failure to obtain that adjustment they have no power or means to redress their loss by imposing the adjustment on the parent company abroad. The use of the advanced pricing method, which involves the agreement of the parent company and its own national

tax authority, may be the solution to this problem, following the establishment of such a mechanism with the Japanese government.'
- 'Staff training to improve auditing and computer skills should be increased.'
- 'With regard to the transfer of tangible assets, it is important to know the prices paid for imported raw materials and parts, as well as the prices obtained for the export of finished products. International cooperation by tax authorities could guarantee this.'
- 'We need to have a better understanding of overseas tax laws. The establishment of a national transfer pricing web to exchange information and experiences and to access overseas tax laws by the use of the web would be a way forward.'
- 'To help in the discovery of transfer pricing manipulations, tax examiners who are involved with other tax liabilities of a company should be alert to the presence of transfer pricing abuses, and be qualified to understand the management and operations of the company as a whole.'

Summary˙

The audit risk level for a company lies substantially in its own hands. The factors which most readily attract the attention of the tax authorities in China are presented in this chapter. Whilst a company may be more exposed than others on account of its given characteristics, it can increase or reduce the risk of an audit by its policies and practices over transfer pricing which produce the many outcomes that attract the notice of the tax authorities.

13
Managing the Audit

Introduction

In this chapter, data on audit policy and practice are assembled from two internal documents, each prepared by a different tax bureau for the purposes of a national conference of tax authorities in China on the subject of anti-tax avoidance work and experience, together with the direct testimony of a head of an anti-tax avoidance office, specifically obtained for this book.

Tax authorities at work

To obtain an understanding of transfer pricing audit practices from the tax authority's overall point of view – in contrast to the inferences that may be drawn from individual company case material – the transfer pricing audit reports of 1998 and 1999 from each of two tax bureaux, located in different major coastal provinces, were collected directly from the tax auditors. They disclose data on the practice of audits regarding transfer pricing in China – in particular, the reasons and grounds for proceeding with an audit. The two provinces concerned are popular destinations for foreign investment and both tax bureaux have established sound tax auditing systems to protect their tax bases from being eroded. The names of the tax bureaux and the provinces remain anonymous, in respect of normal research standards of confidentiality. The two tax bureaux are referred to as tax bureau A and tax bureau B.

Transfer pricing audits of tax bureau A. In 1998, the tax bureau at the provincial level investigated 75 associated enterprises. The adjustments of taxable income of 51 of these enterprises resulted in an additional taxable income of RNB 263.18 million, with a liability to pay RNB 10.34 million, and put 22 companies on a profit making footing. Twenty (39%) were adjusted by adopting the cost plus method, 12 (23.5%) were adjusted by adopting the comparable uncontrolled price method, two (4%) were adjusted by adopting the resale price method, one (2%) was adjusted by adopting the profit split method, another one (2%) was adjusted according to its advance pricing agreement, and fifteen (29.5%) were adjusted by the use of other methods. At the municipal level, 347 enterprises conducted related party transactions, of which 161 were suspected of having manipulated their tax liabilities and were eventually audited.

A record of the development of transfer pricing audit practices of tax bureau A is presented as follows.

1. Developing an anti-avoidance infrastructure and monitoring system. In 1997, an anti-avoidance office of the tax bureau was established at the provincial level. At the beginning of 1998, three levels of the anti-avoidance offices were developed in 17 cities and districts of the province, as follows:

- In those cities and districts with developed economies and a relatively large number of foreign investment enterprises, offices specifically for anti-avoidance were established with more than four tax auditors
- In those cities and districts with a relatively large number of foreign investment enterprises, offices specifically for anti-avoidance were established with more than three tax auditors.
- In those cities and districts with less developed economies and a relatively few number of foreign investment enterprises, offices specifically for anti-avoidance were established with more than two tax auditors.

To monitor multinational transfer pricing behaviour, associated enterprises are grouped into four levels for surveillance purposes as follows:

- Level One: Companies with related party transactions, and are suspected of tax avoidance behaviour, are listed as audit targets
- Level Two: Companies with related party transactions, and are suspected of tax avoidance behaviour, but not listed as audit targets, are noted for future reference

- Level Three: Companies which have been audited but without adjustments
- Level Four: Companies which have been audited and subsequently adjusted.

2. Recruiting and training anti-avoidance auditors. Tax auditors qualify by attending and passing public examinations. The recruitment criteria adopted are that the candidates should have sound knowledge and skills in the field of international tax auditing, a good grasp of English language, and an understanding of the ethical issues governing their duties. The auditors are specifically responsible for organizing and coordinating anti-avoidance activities, and supervising significant audit cases throughout the province. By the end of 1998, there were 38 full-time anti-avoidance auditors and 107 part-time anti-avoidance auditors in the province. In 1998, a series of training classes on anti-avoidance issues were conducted, about 200 auditors attending. Auditor specialists at the State Administration of Taxation and other advanced provinces were invited to conduct training work. This training concentrated on practical case studies, specifically analysing large multinational companies that had been subjected to significant tax adjustments.

3. Carrying out anti-avoidance activities. The audit office requires foreign investment enterprises and foreign enterprises operating in the province to disclose data about their related party transactions on their annual corporate tax returns. Those that fail to meet the requirements are subject to penalties. From the information supplied on these returns, the tax auditors analyse a company's performance by identifying and considering important indicators such as its product sales gross profit margin, and the ratio of revenue to operating expenses, in the light of the profit ratio for the industry at large.

On selecting a company for a transfer pricing audit, the auditors proceed with their work in three broad stages as follows.

1. Desk audit. The tax auditors check a series of company documents such as contracts, programme feasibility reports, financial statements, purchases, and sale bills. In checking the documents, the tax auditor may discover that the company has conducted related party transactions, and if so, whether the intercompany charges or payments are reasonable. As an example, during a routine examination of a packaging company's documents, the tax auditors discovered that in addition to selling its products in the domestic market, the company exported to its overseas associated enterprises. Compared with sales prices in the domestic market, the export prices were much lower at barely 26.3% of the domestic prices, the company reporting continuous losses. The company was therefore audited, the outcome being an adjustment for an assessed additional taxable income of RNB 4.922 million.

2. Examination and evaluation. During the examination and evaluation of the documents supplied by the taxpayer, the tax auditors not only check whether the information supplied by the taxpayer accurately reflects a company's business operations, but also identify companies which are suspected of tax avoidance. For example, the tax auditors found that a construction company reported profits during its tax exemption period, but after the termination of the exemption period, the company reported a series of losses. The tax auditors therefore targeted the company to investigate its suspected tax avoidance behavior. During the document examination and evaluation stage, they discovered that by paying excess consulting fees to its overseas parent company the company had reduced its tax liabilities in China. By reference to the company's normal ratio of sales to expenses, the tax auditors made an adjustment of an additional taxable income of RNB 0.17 million, with a liability to pay RNB 0.03 million additional tax.

3. Tax checks. By comparing a company's performance with the terms of its registered foundation capital and total investment, the tax auditors check if a company reporting lower profits or losses for an extended period simultaneously expands its operations disproportionately to its declared resources. By comparing a company's current performance with those of its previous years, the tax auditors check whether the company has reported sudden and significant drops in profit after the termination of a preferential tax treatment period, such as a tax holiday. By comparing a company's performance with those of companies in the same industry, the tax auditors can check if the company is reporting a lower profitability than the norm for enterprises in the same industry.

For example, the provincial capital city anti-avoidance auditors investigated the gross profit levels of ten foreign-based clothing companies located in the city. They found that, on average, their gross profit margins ranged between 20.74% and 24.47%, but that it was barely

10.39% for one company. For this reason, the company in question was subjected to an audit which resulted in the adjustment of an assessed additional taxable income of RNB 1.91 million, with a liability to pay RNB 0.46 million extra tax. In another case, during a tax examination the tax auditors discovered that an electrical goods company reported constant losses, but that 90% of its purchases and sales transactions were conducted with its overseas associated companies. This company was suspected of having manipulated its tax liabilities. The tax auditors made an adjustment of an additional taxable income of RNB 9.89 million, which put the company into a profit making position.

Transfer pricing audits of tax bureau B. In 1999, tax bureau B investigated 67 associated enterprises. The adjustments of taxable income of 58 of these enterprises resulted in an assessed additional taxable income of RNB 337 million, with a collective liability to pay RNB 18.36 million. The transfer pricing audit practices of tax bureau B are presented as follows.

Desk audit. By examining a series of company documents such as tax returns, contracts, program feasibility reports, financial statements, purchases and sale bills, the tax auditor may uncover whether the company has conducted related party transactions, and if so, whether the transactions are based upon the arm's length principle.

Examination and evaluation. By examining and evaluating a targeted company, the tax auditors can discover whether the company has disclosed its related party transactions, and if it has been guilty of tax avoidance behaviour. In an analysis of the financial position and results of operations of a company, the tax auditors take eight economic indicators into account. These include: ratio of debts to assets, ratio of current assets to current liquidities, ratio of quick assets (inventory) to current liabilities, receivable turnover ratio, inventory turnover ratio, ratio of profits to capital, ratio of profits to sales, and ratio of profits to costs and charges.

In 1999, the tax auditors operating throughout the province between them examined and evaluated the trading records – submitted by them as required with their annual tax returns – of 20,000 companies in the province. Of these companies, the managers of 2,000 were ordered to provide the data for their intercompany trading and transfer pricing.

This province has the standard structure for tax collection. The tax bureau at the provincial level oversees the many local tax bureaux, each of which is responsible for a city and its environs – either alone, or in conjunction with one other or more bureaux, according to the size of the city. It is usual for the provincial office to deal with larger companies and cases of complexity. Local tax bureaux handle small companies and straightforward cases. For this particular year, eventually 67 companies were audited by the provincial office alone, 58 receiving adjustments as a result of perceived transfer pricing abuses.

One of these cases – previously featured briefly in Chapter 11 – is presented as follows in more detail. A Sino-Japanese Wholly Owned Subsidiary was established in 1995 in a major city of the province as an Equity Joint Venture, with a paid-in capital of US$ 170,000 to manufacture and sell cartoon films with a projected production life of eleven years. In 1996, however, the company was put on a new footing as a Wholly Owned Company. The raw materials were imported from abroad. The parent company was also responsible for designing the contents of the cartoons, whereas the Chinese subsidiary only processed and made the final products.

The tax auditors identified the following four issues during their investigation.

- The company opened in May 1995. It reported yearly losses from then to 1998, losses being posted as RNB 500,000 for 1995, RNB 66,000 for 1996, RNB 223,000 for 1997, and RNB 218,000 for 1998, totaling over RNB 1 million
- Over these years its annual profit rate was minus 24.1%, whereas its feasibility report anticipated 23.33%, the average annual profit rate for the industry at large being 10%
- The prices paid for raw materials and for product output were controlled by the parent company. Both the raw materials involved and the output itself were channeled through the parent company, the former being obtained from international markets and the latter being sold internationally
- Over the period 1995 to 1998, sales revenue increased from RMB 700,000 to RMB 2.3 million. However, the company reported losses during those years
- In analysing the company's financial position and results of operations, the tax auditors found that the company held 719.28% and 608.39% of the receivable turnover ratio and inventory turnover ratio, which were positive, but on average, its ratio of profits to capital, ratio of profits to sales, ratio of profits to costs and charges, were minus 32.65%, minus 24.1%, and minus 16.1% respectively, which were negative.

Given the issues identified, in 1998, the company was targeted for suspected tax avoidance behaviour. The tax authority, being unable to obtain the prices ultimately charged by the parent company, was unable to apply the resale price method, and was therefore obliged to use the comparable uncontrolled price method to adjust the company's tax liability when it subjected the company to an audit. It compared this company's reported figures with those of a Taiwanese company with a similar product sold to the Japanese company that had no association with it.

The auditors identified seven common points between the Chinese and Taiwanese companies:

- Both made the same product, that is, the cartoon films
- Both conducted the same functions: The Japanese company designed the product and supplied the raw materials but they were processed by the Chinese and Taiwanese companies
- Both held the same sales terms: The Japanese company was responsible for the sale of the final products in the Japanese market. Both the Chinese and Taiwanese companies bore no risks
- Both imported the same raw materials with similar prices and of similar quality from the Japanese company
- Employed workers had the same skills
- The date of transactions was the same for both – the period 1995 to 1998.

As a result of the audit, the company's combined taxable income for the years 1996 and 1997 was adjusted to RNB 3,449,343.7, with a consequent extra tax payment of RNB 70,649.21.

Personal viewpoint

Specifically for this book In December 2005, the head of the Anti-Tax Avoidance Office of a major tax bureau of a coastal city presented an overview of the audit work carried out by his office. A staff of six specialist auditors for transfer pricing carry out the audit work of the office, as part of a large tax bureau which has several specialist departments. It operates both directly within its own area but in addition oversees the work of a score of subsidiary bureaux that respectively handle the administration of tax affairs in their allotted areas of the city itself and the country district areas outside of it. The taxes collected from foreign companies by this bureau are value added tax, consumption tax, business tax, income tax, and resource tax. His own office was established in 1998, in common with the establishment of many other such offices throughout China to cope with transfer pricing abuses. Many cities now have well established audit systems, especially in the eastern coastal cities Shenzhen, Qingdao, Tianjin, Shanghai, Guangzhou, Xiamen, Dalian, and Nanjing.

His field of responsibilities includes the organization of the specialist staff and their duties, and the coordination of their work to ensure the coverage of the whole city. His office functions to ensure that companies comply with the laws on taxation in the course of making intercompany transactions. He is responsible for collecting taxes levied and in particular the additional taxes for which companies become liable following re-assessments and adjustments arising from audits. He takes part in the training of auditors for his own and other authorities. Each year his office draws up a list of companies that will be audited, the choice being based on an examination of the initial documentation received with a company's annual tax return and the definitions of affiliation as laid down by the State Administration of Taxation. His reports on the conduct, activities, and findings of his office, made regularly to the State Administration of Taxation, contribute with those from similar officers throughout China to the overall record of taxation in practice and the formulation of legislative and administrative changes as necessary.

It is constant work to identify recalcitrant companies and prepare them for audit. The cost plus is normally a simple and easy method to use for audit wherever possible, using industry standards as the benchmark, and is readily understood by the taxpayer. This method needs the collection of comparable data from elsewhere – such as the internet and the embassies – to establish a company's relative position in a range of financial and accounting variables within those known for the industry as a whole.

His office normally classifies companies that are under suspicion into three categories. The first group includes those that have been previously audited but have reformed, basing their transfer pricing according to the arm's length principle. As long as the profit levels of these companies remain normal, they are not subject to an audit again. The second group consists of previously audited companies that have maintained their adjusted price levels but are showing expenditure in excess of that of income. These companies are listed for a further audit. The third group are the companies that have been previously audited but have failed to comply with the requirements imposed. The concealed and unlawful income obtained by these companies in excess of the amounts obtainable for the same transactions with unrelated companies is regarded as a dividend payment. This deemed dividend is not entitled to the privilege of exemption from income tax.

His office concentrates on larger companies, and manufacturing companies – especially those in electronics, telecommunications, together with garments, plastics, and reprocessing or finishing work. The notable signs of malpractice are a state of long-term losses or low profits but the simultaneous expansion of operations or fluctuating profits. Signs that draw a company to his attention are the import of raw materials at high prices from a parent company or foreign associates and the export of products to them at low prices. This particular set of circumstances was illustrated by the tax official in the following case.

A Taiwanese Wholly Owned Subsidiary audited in 2005
- Background of the case

The Taiwanese Wholly Owned Subsidiary was established in 2000, with a projected production life of 30 years, manufacturing and selling hardware products. The parent company supplies all the raw materials through its agency in Hong Kong and authorizes the Chinese subsidiary in return to sell its product direct to the agency in response to the orders for sales that are transmitted to the subsidiary from the parent company via the agency. Customers pay this agency direct for their purchases and the agency then reimburses the subsidiary, as shown in Figure 13.1.

- Issues detected

During the period 2000 to 2005, the company reported accumulated losses of RMB 9.73 million. Raw materials were purchased through, and final products sold to, the Hong Kong agency, respectively at purchase prices higher and sales prices lower than those in the domestic market.

- Selection of the method and adjustments

The tax authority adjusted the company's taxable income by using the cost plus method. Many Taiwanese companies, instead of investing directly, invest in China via Hong Kong. It is estimated that if investments were traced back to their true origins, Taiwan might well turn out to be the largest investor in China. China's top 200 export companies are headed by Taiwanese-based information technology firms. The company's strategy in this case clearly illustrates the prominent advantage that can be taken of the prevailing low tax rates in Hong Kong.

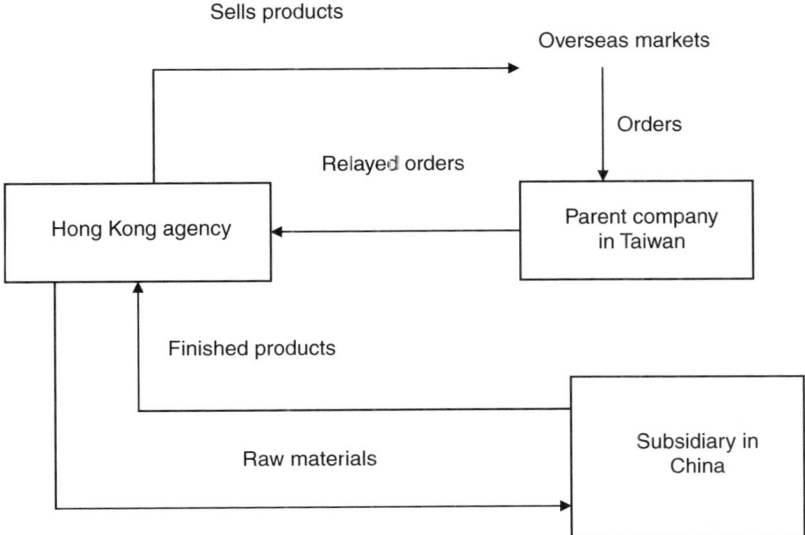

Figure 13.1 Transaction flows for the exemplary audit case

Summary

The general procedures for arriving at a list of companies to be audited and the actual conduct of audits themselves are laid down as standard requirements by the State Administration of Taxation, but local tax authorities are empowered to exercise a degree of discretion, provided the main rules of procedure are observed. The sheer scale of the task of monitoring company operations to prevent transfer pricing abuses is daunting for the tax authorities, particularly in the areas where foreign direct investment and foreign enterprises are most concentrated. As well as the size of the task, however, the structural and relational possibilities – devised and used by companies to conceal their transfer pricing deceptions – exacerbate the difficulties of detection and treatment. Although an increase of staff, the qualitative enhancement of staff, and mechanical aids have characterised the response of the authorities to the need, the fact remains that the means of control are not commensurate with the task, deficiencies which are expressed in the frustrations experienced by individual members of staff in the course of their work.

14
Audits in Future

Introduction

This book offers an introduction to, and overview of, transfer pricing audits in China. It consists firstly of a reference to the commercial landscape of the current world economy as it affects and is manifested in China, an explanation of the nature and purposes of transfer pricing, and the laws and regulations which worldwide authorities have put in place to curb the transfer pricing malpractice which deprives national governments of their legitimate tax revenues. There follows a range of topics covering the attitudes of foreign investment companies to transfer pricing and their uses of it, the organization, extent and procedural steps involved in the audit of a foreign investment enterprise operating in China, together with case studies and the views and comments of tax officials concerned with audit work, special reference being made to the company characteristics and practices which are most likely to invite the attention of the tax authorities and a consequent audit.

This final chapter endeavours to highlight current features and potentials which can suggest the developments that will take place, some on the basis of promise and commitment, others on the basis of inference and speculation.

Development markers

Towards the end of 2005, Wei Jianguo, the Chinese Vice-Minister of Commerce, claimed that 450 of the World's Top 500 companies had invested in China. The claim was made during a conference for China's private businesses and the World's Top 500 firms in

Hangzhou, capital of east China's booming Zhejiang Province. At the same conference, Liu Yajun, Director of the Investment Promotion Department under the Ministry of Commerce, asserted that China had been improving its investment environment in recent years, while foreign investors had been optimizing their investment structures. Businessmen from 202 countries had invested in China during 2005, involving US$ 600 billion, and covering almost all fields of economic activity, including services, manufacturing, and rural infrastructure construction, but with special emphasis on the high-technology and trade services industries, with electronics, automotive, and chemical industries also featuring strongly. Such overseas investment had contributed greatly to China's economic growth. The industrial added value of joint-venture origin formed about 27.8% of the national industrial added value, joint ventures contributing about 20.8% of the national revenue and generating about 20 million jobs in 2005 (Xinhua, 2005).

Monumental developments of these orders of magnitude, impressive as they are in global terms, and dramatic as their practical effects are in China itself which they represent, must be seen in terms of the potential they carry for future changes to the industrial and commercial life of China – and indeed to the entire conditions and cultural characteristics of China. Both benefits and ills are in the offing.

Writing in the *China Daily* (12 August 2005, p. 44), Fu Jing reported that a cabinet think-tank has suggested that China should introduce an early warning system to prevent multinational companies from cornering the Chinese market. Xie Fuzhan, Vice-President of the State Council Development Research Centre has urged the government to take action against foreign investors who have intensified their expansion in some industrial sectors and have obtained sizeable shares, if not a quasi-monopolistic interest – a remark prompted no doubt by the fact that their involvement in some large projects has increased considerably this year. 'These are new trends in foreign investment, and they deserve close attention,' he warned, 'although they should not be allowed to conflict with our lasting strategy that emphasizes partnerships with multinational companies which are willing to transfer core technologies and management experience.' In facing the new investment trend, it was suggested that China should establish standards and a system to monitor the behaviour of overseas investors to prevent monopoly risks for the Chinese domestic market, in accord with the Anti-Monopoly Law, which is due for consideration and decision by the National People's Congress in the near future.

According to Lin Yueqin, researcher at the Chinese Academy of Social Sciences, in addition to preventing foreign investors from implementing monopolistic practices, China is seeking to establish a law to create equal market access for all investors, which will stipulate very clearly that a dominant market position should not be abused by any company operating in a particular market, irrespective of its domestic or foreign origin. In future, in permitting but limiting mergers and acquisitions, China will create a report system requiring that proposed mergers or acquisitions meet certain criteria to obtain approval. These criteria will be publicly transparent, meaning that enterprises will be held fully responsible for their business activities.

In terms of the inflow of foreign direct investment, China ranks second to the United States, which received US$ 96 billion in 2004, according to a United Nations report. During the January–October period of 2005, foreign direct investment in China reached US$ 48.4 billion, currently averaging US$ 4.04 million per contract, up from US$ 3.51 million in 2004. A new trend is that instead of forging partnerships with local companies, foreign enterprises are increasing their efforts to become single investors in China.

Many foreign companies, which mainly operate factories and processing plants in China, are moving their research and development departments to China, over 700 foreign research and development laboratories having been set up in China since Motorola established the first one in 1993. The latest prominent company to do so is Ericsson, the world's largest maker of mobile phone networks, which announced in September 2005 that it would invest US$ 1 billion in manufacturing and research in China over the next five years.

Managing audit risks

As the State Administration of Taxation is focusing its legislative, regulative and enforcement efforts on transfer pricing practices, the chances that foreign investment enterprises will have to face a transfer pricing audit are increasing. It is imperative now for taxpayers to seek effective ways to manage the transfer pricing audit risks. Recommendations to taxpayers on how to design a successful transfer pricing strategy are as follows.

Establishing an appropriate transfer pricing policy. The company must be aware that in developing its pricing policy it must be able to demonstrate to the tax authorities that the transfer prices conform to the arm's length principle. As the substance of transactions is changing constantly, transfer prices must also be changed to remain of arm's length in nature. The transfer pricing policy must be regularly reviewed and amended to ensure that it remains effectively so. Furthermore, it may be advisable to find an independent expert to help to set the transfer pricing in accordance with the tax rules, once the company has established its transactions strategy.

Preparing and maintaining sufficient documentation. Transfer pricing documentation is needed to provide a corporate overview of, and explanation for, the process, and considerations taken into account, for calculating the arm's length pricing of its related party transactions. To avoid disputes or penalties, preparing and maintaining sufficient documentation is crucial. To prove to the tax authorities that the transfer pricing policy is of an arm's length in nature, the documentation should demonstrate that the taxpayer has selected the most reliable method and has applied it in an appropriate manner in respect of all transfer pricing arrangements. In other words, if the transfer pricing policy is sufficiently documented and made available to the tax authorities, then the risk of a detailed transfer pricing audit and the likelihood of transfer pricing adjustments can be avoided or mitigated.

Considering an advance pricing agreement. The advance pricing agreement programme provides an important mechanism for taxpayers to obtain certainty that their transfer pricing policies and procedures meet the requirements of the arm's length standard. One proactive way to reduce the risk of transfer pricing audits imposed by the tax authorities, and possible adjustments, is therefore to apply for an advance pricing agreement. An advance pricing agreement is a binding legal agreement between the taxpayer and the tax authority. This device is clearly to the advantage of the tax authority. It guarantees that tax will be collected but as has been highlighted elsewhere in this book, the binding nature of the contract may chafe against the entrepreneurial spirit and smack of concealed state control.

At the present time there is insufficient long-term experience of advance pricing agreements in China to assess their utility and acceptability to contracting companies. In prospect the advance pricing agreement looks daunting, both on account of the documentary preparations needed for it, and its constricting nature. But if the precedents set by all manner of such regulatory devices in human experience are anything to go by, it is at least possible that in future a company could learn to live with its advance pricing agreement and still be able to find ways to circumvent its restrictions, if not actually to undermine it. The struggle in economic life to impose restrictions on others while obtaining freedom for oneself will certainly continue, although the burgeoning nature of economic growth of China makes it unusually difficult to ascertain the certainties and uncertainties for the near future. Table 14.1 offers a commentary on this statement.

The one certain feature of future commercial activity in China is that transfer pricing will be manipulated in one way or another for the purpose of tax avoidance and evasion. With all China's determination to confront this prevalent affront to its trading laws and deprivation of its just taxation revenues, the fact remains that the practice is an entrenched condition of commercial life on a vast scale. The low respect for law in general and the endemic habit of tax avoidance and evasion by the indigenous population presents nothing if not a breeding ground for the practice to prosper. China is not and will not be alone over this issue. Every country in the world which to one extent or another participates in the international commercial activities of the global economy is prey to the same disability. Each country's laws simultaneously present inhibitions and opportunities for business transactions involving a second country. The entire activity represented by international trading provides for the sustenance and wellbeing of the world's population. Its

Table 14.1   Anticipated changes in trading conditions in China

Factor	Past	Future
Company size	Medium/Smaller Companies	+ Larger Companies
Company country of origin	Hong Kong, Taiwan, Japan	+ Western countries, tax havens
Transaction types subject to audit	Tangible goods	+ Intangible goods, services, and finance
Attitude of tax offices to transfer price	Not important	Crucial to tax collection
Advance pricing agreement	Unilateral	+ Bilateral and Multilateral
Laws for transfer pricing	Simple	Comprehensive
Tax Rates	Differentiated	Common to all companies
Policy	Attracting capital	Controlling company power

necessary existence generates irregularities which have to be tolerated because they cannot be eliminated, but may be mitigated within the bounds of economic effort that can be afforded. In China's case the audit will become its main tool for combating malpractice.

With regard to transfer pricing audits, therefore, three propositions are advanced as indicative of the way ahead.

1. The scope for transfer pricing audits in China will increase
   - by increasing the numbers targeted further into the range of existing companies
   - by needing to cope with additional new foreign investment enterprises
   - by having to deal with a greater spectrum of types of business activity
2. The audit capacity and competence of a tax authority's staff will improve
   - the number of specialist staff is being increased
   - the experience of staff is deepening
   - the international cooperation between tax authorities is developing
3. A countervailing movement is likely to appear in multinational company practice
   - ever more subtle and devious means for concealing transactions will be found
   - more skilled accounting and financial staff will be employed
   - new ways for enterprise units to be associated will be fashioned.

Statistics indicate that intercompany transactions among multinational enterprises now account for about one-third of total world trade. About 80% of the payments for the transfer of technology is through related party transactions. China has been open house to foreign investment enterprises – particularly with a view to importing the full range of the technologies of worldwide industries. At first, foreign investment enterprises which were home-based in countries with high tax rates and high wage rates were quick to take advantage of the opportunities existing in China by way of lower labour rates and lower technology levels. During the 1990s, industries employing higher levels of technology made their presence felt. Since the turn of the century service industries have joined the economy and account for about one-third of contracted foreign investment.

It remains the case that, by whatever criteria are used to measure the disparities, the huge incursion of foreign investment enterprises is concentrated in the eastern parts of the country, as opposed to the central and western parts, although evidence of the increasing location of foreign investment enterprises in central areas of China is to hand. This latter fact suggests that foreign companies are finding it attractive to locate in these central areas to take advantage of their differential wage rates, land charges, and transportation costs, and other economies in serving localized markets. The arrival of service and retail firms have probably accentuated this development. By the same token it may be assumed that the movement westwards beyond the central areas will sooner or later continue.

Whilst joint venture and joint exploration were the predominant modes of commitment for foreign investment enterprises in the early days of the transformation of China's domestic economic policy, equity joint venture and wholly owned legal forms were preferred during the late 1980s. During the following decade, however, the wholly owned enterprise became dominant – and foreign control of the joint venture increased as the government relaxed the regulations controlling the terms for forming and operating it. In any case, foreign companies gradually became familiar with China's culture and economic environment to the extent that eventually they felt at home in China and became fully competent in their own right. Foreign companies were thus able to pour in more investment capital – in particular in exclusive high technology industries which China welcomed and which helped to create new industrial dimensions and competitive markets for China's economy.

As foreign direct investment increases in future, the United States and the European Union will take a higher proportionate share of the total investment, wholly owned firms being in the ascendant. Whilst the availability of low labour costs may tempt companies to locate further westwards, away from the concentrations of foreign firms in coastal locations, high technology industries are likely to continue to increase their presence in those areas, fuelling China's economic growth still further. Long established companies within China may well be tempted into mergers and new networks of affiliation. The recent reduction of prohibitive regulations that limited the type of business which foreign investment enterprises may run in China will see an ever widening spectrum of business activities covering the entire field of commercial activities characteristic of the developed countries.

In conclusion

The economic transformation of China is a phenomenon of the first order. The development of the United States over a period of 300 years carried that country to its present dominance and unprecedented levels of achievement. The development of Japan took some 150 years to carry the country to the position of being the world's second economy. In 30 years China has emerged from economic obscurity to become potentially the world's leading economy. Telescoped into this short time has been some of the experiences and processes of economic development that have had the benefit of a much longer maturation period in other countries. China has reaped the benefit of the accumulated knowledge and skills and capital that have been more slowly gathered elsewhere. It is unlikely to squander them. Its indigenous inventiveness and energy of historic fame will surely capitalize on the vast investments that it has invited from other countries to supplement its own assets.

Bibliography

Abdallah, W.M. (2004). *Critical concerns in transfer pricing and practice.* Westport CT: Praeger.

Atkinson, M. and Tyrrall, D. (1999). *International transfer pricing: A practical guide for finance directors.* London: Financial Times Management/Pearson Education.

Belkaoui, A. (1991). *Multinational management accounting.* NY: Quorum Books.

Borkowski, S.C. (1996). Advance pricing (dis)agreements: Differences in tax authority and transnational corporation opinions. *International Tax Journal*, 22(3), 23–34.

Buckley, P.J. and Casson, M. (1976). *The future of the multinational enterprise.* London: Macmillan.

Caves, R. (ed.) (1996). *Multinational enterprise and economic analysis* (2nd ed.). Cambridge, England: Cambridge University Press.

Chan, K. and Chow, L. (1998). *International transfer pricing in China.* Hong Kong: Sweet and Maxwell Asia.

Cho, S. (ed.). (1998). *Taxation reforms in China.* Hong Kong: Hong Kong Polytechnic University.

Chong, S. and De Souza, G. (2005). *China transfer pricing – Important and new developments.* Price Waterhouse, October.

Coase, R.H. (1937). The nature of the firm. London: *Economica.*

Corley, T.A.B. (1992). John Dunning's contribution to international business studies. In P. Buckley and M. Casson (eds), *Multinational Enterprises in the World Economy: Essays in Honour of John Dunning* (pp. 1–19). London: Edward Elgar Publishing.

Deloitte (2006). *Strategy Matrix for Global Transfer Pricing,* Deloitte.

De Souza, G.R. (2003). *Introduction to U.S. transfer pricing,* PricewaterhouseCoopers.

Dunning, J.H. (1980). Toward an eclectic theory of international production. *Journal of International Business Studies,* 11(Spring/Summer), 9–31.

Dunning, J.H. and Rugman, A.M. (1985). The influence of Hymer's dissertation on the theory of foreign direct investment. *American Economic Review,* 75, May, 228–232.

Eichelberger, J., Levey, M., and Tao, P. (2005). China – Racing to catch up with global transfer pricing standards, *International Tax Review,* Supplement: Asia transfer pricing, October.

Ernst and Young (2003). *Transfer pricing 2003 global survey.* London: Ernst and Young International.

Ernst and Young (2004a). *PRC client alert – The SAT issues private ruling on research and development cost sharing arrangements,* Issue 6, December.

Ernst and Young (2004b). *Transfer pricing 2004 global survey.* London: Ernst and Young International.

Fu, J. (2005). Foreign firms' monopolies cause concern. *China Daily,* 12 August.

Harrison, J. and Glyn-Jones, A. (1999). *Transfer pricing handbook: A practical guide for New Zealand business.* Auckland, New Zealand: CCH New Zealand.

Hines, J.R. and Rice, E.M. (1994). Fiscal paradise: Foreign tax havens and American business. *Journal of Economics*, 109(1), 149–182.

Hymer, S.H. (1976). *The international operations of national firms: A study of direct foreign investment*. Cambridge, MA: MIT Press.

Invest in China (2005). *Foreign direct investment from the top ten countries to December 2004*. Beijing: Author (in Chinese). Retrieved October 17, 2005 from http://www.fdi.gov.cn

Invest in China (2005). *Regional distribution of actual foreign direct investment to December 2004*. Beijing: Author (in Chinese). Retrieved February 1, 2005 from http://www.fdi.gov.cn

Invest in China (2005). *Portions of China's total exports and imports contributed by foreign investment enterprises (FIEs) 1990–2004*. Beijing: Author (in Chinese). Retrieved February 1, 2005 from http://www.fdi.gov.cn

Invest in China (2005). *Exports by foreign investment enterprises to the main countries or other destinations, 1991–1994*. Beijing: Author (in Chinese). Retrieved February 1, 2005 from http://www.fdi.gov.cn

Invest in China (2005). *Imports by foreign investment enterprises from the main countries or other sources, 1991–1994*. Beijing: Author (in Chinese). Retrieved February 1, 2005 from http://www.fdi.gov.cn

Kindleberger, C.P. (1984). *Multinational excursions*. Cambridge, MA: MIT Press.

Klopfer, J. Peters, D., and Waldens, S. (2005). The challenge to align operational and legal transfer pricing. *International Tax Review*, Supplement: transfer pricing, July.

Lai, P.Y. (2002). Foreign direct investment in China: Recent trends and patterns. *China & World Economy*, No 2.

Lee, J., Xiao, W., and Kuo, D. (2004). *Overview of China's impending APA rules*. Deloitte: Issue HK 02/04, March.

Li, J. and Paisey, A. (2005). *International transfer pricing in Asia Pacific: Perspectives on trade between Australia, New Zealand and China*. London: Palgrave Macmillan.

Ministry of Commerce of the People's Republic of China (2004). *Foreign direct investment in China*. Beijing: Author (in Chinese). Retrieved January 11, 2004 from http://www.mofcom.gov.cn

Ministry of Commerce of the People's Republic of China (2004). *Forms of foreign direct investment to December 2004*. Beijing: Author (in Chinese). Retrieved January 11, 2004 from http://www.mofcom.gov.cn

Ministry of Commerce of the People's Republic of China (2004). *Income tax rates of some of China's main trading partners*. Beijing: Author (in Chinese). Retrieved January 11, 2004 from http://www.mofcom.gov.cn

Mo, P.L. (2003). *Tax avoidance and anti-avoidance measures in major developing economies*. Westport, Conn: Praeger.

OECD, Organisation for Economic Cooperation and Development, Committee on Fiscal Affairs (1995). *Transfer pricing guidelines for multinational enterprises and tax administrations*. Paris: OECD Publications.

PricewaterhouseCoopers (2004). *Latest regulatory development of advance pricing arrangements in China*. Autumn.

PricewaterhouseCoopers (2005). *Revised transfer pricing regulations: More strengthened and centralized transfer pricing enforcement in China*. February.

Rolfe, C. (ed.) (1997). *International transfer pricing: 1997–98*. London: CCH Editions Limited.
SAT, the State Administration of Taxation (1998). Guo Shui Fa (No. 59): Tax administration rules and procedures for transactions between related parties. Beijing: SAT.
SAT, the State Administration of Taxation (2004). Guo Shui Fa (No. 118): Implementation rules for advance pricing arrangements for transactions between related parties. Beijing: SAT.
SAT, the State Administration of Taxation (2005). Guo Shui Fa (No. 115): Implementing mutual agreement procedures. Beijing: SAT.
Sun, H.S. (1999). DFI, foreign trade and transfer pricing. *Journal of Contemporary Asia*, 29(3), 362–382.
The world's top 500 multinational companies operating in China. (2nd ed.) (2003). ShangDong, China: People's Publisher of ShangDong (in Chinese).
Tomsett, E. (1989). *Tax planning for multinational companies*. NY: Woodhood-Faulkner Publishers.
Tseng, S. and Lee, J. (2005). Transfer pricing challenges in China. *International Tax Review*, Supplement: transfer pricing, July.
Vernon, R. (1971). *Sovereignty at Bay*. NY: Basic Books.
Wei, S. (2004). *New transfer pricing development in China*, Deloitte: Issue HK 03/04, July.
Wei, S. (2004). *A step towards contemporaneous documentation requirement*. Deloitte: Issue HK 04/04, August.
Xinhua (2005). Four hundred and fifty of the world's top 500 companies have invested in China. *Xinhua*, December.
Zhao, Y. (2002). Transfer pricing. *International Tax Review*, Supplement: 42–48.

Index

Acceptable pricing methods, 35–6, 48–9
Adjustment methods, 34–5, 69–81
 selection of, 78–9, 153
Adjustment of income by audit, 106, 160–1, 163–4
Advance pricing agreements, 37, 38–9, 50, 90–9, 131, 173–4
 applying for, 92, 94
 bilateral agreement for, 90
 case in point for, 90–1
 confidentiality of, 96–7
 criteria for, 93–4
 definition of, 90
 drafting of, 95
 evaluation of, 94–5
 execution of, 96
 monitoring of, 96
 negotiation for, 95
 opportunities for, 97–9
 pitfalls of, 97–9
 pre-file meeting for, 93–4
 review of, 94–5
 signing of, 96
 time limit for, 96
Anti-Monopoly Law, 171
Appeals procedure, 107
Arm's length principle, 34, 69–71, 134
 definition of, 70
 illustration of, 70
Associated enterprises, 48, 50, 56–68, 101–4
 defined, 48
 illustration of, 63
 meaning of, 61–2
 organizational structure of, 63
Audit adjustment methods, 71–8
Audit in Action, 104–11, 134–48, 160–8
 cases of, 109–10, 131–3, 134–48, 163–6, 168–9
 finance case of, 144–5
 intangible goods case of, 142–4

 services case of, 144
 tangible goods cases of, 134–42
Audit policy and practice development, 157–9, 170, 174–5
Audit Risk Levels, 151–2
 conditional factors affecting, 154–5
 model of, 153–6
 personal perspectives of tax officials of, 149–51, 166–9
 tax authority perspectives of, 151–3
 volitional factors affecting, 155
Audit targets, identification of, 104–5
Audits,
 criteria for incurring, 151–2
 development markers for future of, 174
 managing the risks of, 172–5
 recommendations for avoiding, 172–3
Australian approach to documentation, 84–5
Autonomous Regions, 11
 Guangxi, 11
 Inner Mongolia, 11
 Ningxia, 11
 Tibet, 11
 Xinjiang, 11

Beijing, 11
Burden of proof, 38, 49, 83, 105–6

Canada, 33, 39–40
Capital structure, 20
Cases of transfer pricing audits, 134–45
 finance, 144–5
 intangible goods, 142–4
 services, 144
 tangible goods, 134–42
Central region, 11
China Daily, 171
China's rules, 45–8
 burden of proof in, 49

Index

China's rules – *continued*
  penalties in, 49
  preferred methods in, 48–9
  required documentation by, 49
China's transfer pricing regime, 48–50
Chinese,
  Academy of Social Sciences, 172
  courts, 107
  imports and exports, 14–17
  income tax, 27
  levels of foreign direct investment, 172
  taxes, 26–30
  tax officials, 108, 149–51, 160
  tax bureaux, 108–10, 160–6
Chongqing, 11
Coastal Open Cities, 30
Coastal Open Economic Zones, 30
Company international tax planning, 18–20
Company registration, 149
Company track records, 155
  as apostates, 156
  as incorrigibles, 156
  as perfectionists, 155–6
  as repentants, 156
Comparability analysis, 93
Comparable profit method, 35, 77
  model of, 77
Comparable uncontrolled method, 34, 71–2
  model of, 72, 73
Competitive advantages, 5–6
Configuration advantages, 6
Conglomerate business, 61
Contemporary audit system, 101–12
  operational data of, 108–10
  procedures in, 101–8, 112
  structure and practice of, 108
Coordinating advantages, 6
Cost plus method, 34–5, 74
  model of, 74–5
Cost sharing agreement, 88
Current transfer pricing rules, 33–43

Dalian, 167
Designated Provincial Capitals, 30
Direct foreign investment,
  foreign trade as, 3–4
  theories of, 4–7
  trends and patterns in China of, 7–17
Divisionalized multi-product business, 57–9
Documentation, 36–7, 38, 49, 83–8
  Australian approach to, 84–5
  current requirements of, 83–4, 86–8
  maintenance of, 85, 173
Double taxation, 79–81, 133
  illustration of, 80–1

Eastern Region, 11
Eclectic paradigm, 5–7
Economic analysis, 94
Economic and Technological
  Development Zones, 30
Ericsson, 172
European Union, 17, 176

Factors affecting transfer pricing, 120–6
  competitive position of subsidiary, 121–2
  comply with tax laws and regulations, 121
  corporate profit of subsidiary, 121
  differences in income tax rates, 124–5
  existence of local partner, 123
  foreign currency exchange controls, 124
  good relations with host government, 122
  import restrictions, 125
  maintenance of cash flows, 122
  overall profit to multinational group, 122
  performance evaluation, 122–3
  political and social pressures, 125–6
  pricing controls of host governments, 125–6
  rates of customs duties, 121
  restrictions on repatriation of income, 123
  royalty restrictions, 125
  tax authority transfer pricing audits, 125
Field audits,
  number of, 108, 160–5

Financial assets, 68
  case of transfer pricing audit on, 144–5
Fines and charges, 89
Foreign company practice,
  data on, 116
  factors affecting transfer pricing in, 120–6
  organizational and environmental variable rankings in, 126–7
  statistical references for research into, 127–31
  transfer pricing methods used in, 117–20
Foreign direct investment, 26
  and foreign trade, 14–17
  as part of China's trade, 7–8, 14–17
  distribution of, 10, 11–12
  distribution according to industry of, 12–14
  exports and imports from, 16–17
  legal forms of, 8–9
  sources of, 9–11
  theories of, 4–7
  trends and patterns in China of, 7–14
Foreign tax credits, 26, 30
France, 33, 40–1
Fu Jing, 171
Fujian, 10
Functional analysis, 76, 86–8, 93

G7, 33, 44
Germany, 33, 41–2
Global formulary apportionment, 35
Globalization, 1, 17, 33, 69
Guangdong, 10
Guangxi, 11
Guangzhou, 167

Hangzhou, 11
Henan, 11
Hong Kong, 9, 17, 27, 133
Hubei, 11
Hunan, 11

Import duties, 25, 28
Income tax, 27
Inner Mongolia, 11

Intangible assets, 65–6
  case of transfer pricing audits on, 142–4
Intercompany international transfers, 115–19
  nature and frequency of, 117
  transfer pricing methods used for, 117–20
  transfer pricing tax audits on, 120
  volume of, 115–19
Italy, 33, 42

Japan, 17, 33, 43
Jiangsu, 10, 29
Joint Ventures, 8, 176
  contractual, 8
  equity, 8
  explorations, 8

Legislation, 133
Lin Yueqin, 172
Liu Yajun, 171

Management fees, 29–30
Managing the Audit,
  personal viewpoint of, 166–8
  tax authorities at work in, 160–6
Market imperfections, 6–7
Mergers and acquisitions, 171–2
Methods, 71–8
  acceptable, 78
  selecting adjustment alternative, 106
Motorola, 12, 172
Multinational enterprises, 3
  capital structure of, 20
  choice of organization by, 20
  deferred foreign income by, 20
  defined, 19
  objectives of, 19
  tax management perspective of, 21–6
  top 500 of, 11, 13–14
Multinational tax management perspective, 21–3
Municipalities,
  Bejing, 11
  Chongqing, 11
  Shanghai, 11
  Tianjun, 11

Nanjing, 167
National People's Congress, 171
Ningxia, 11

OECD, 33, 62
  transfer pricing Guidelines, 35–7
Office auditing,
  number of cases of, 105, 109–11
Organizational structures, 20, 56–61
  conglomerate business, 61
  divisionalised multi-product
    business, 57–9
  single focus business, 57
  vertically integrated business,
    59–60
Ownership tests, 62

Penalties, 36–7, 49–50
Profit split method, 36, 75–7
  model of, 75–61
Provincial Departments, 11

Qingdao, 167

Regions of China,
  Central, 10–12
  Eastern, 10–12
  Western, 10–12
Related parties, 61–8, 101–4
  identity of, 61–4, 101–4
  transactions of, 64
Resale price method, 34, 72–3
  model of, 73–4
Research and development
  investment, 12–13
Revised assessments, 107–8
Royalties, 25, 29, 133
Rules of trading partners,
  Canada, 39–40
  France, 40–1
  Germany, 41–2
  Italy, 42
  Japan, 43
  OECD Guidelines, 35–7
  United Kingdom, 43–4
  United States, 37–9

Selecting the transfer pricing method,
  78–9, 153

Services assets, 67
  case of transfer pricing audits on,
    144
Shanghai, 11, 167
  Pudong New Areas, 30
Shanxi, 10
Share companies with foreign
  investments, 8
Shenzhou, 167
Sichuan, 10
Siemens Corporation, 3
Single focus business, 57
Special Economic Zones, 30
Suzhou, 29

Taiwan, 17
Tangible assets, 65
  cases of transfer pricing audits on,
    134–42
Tax audit procedures, 101–11, 112,
  162–6
Tax authorities at work, 160–9
  anti-avoidance activities of, 161–2
  infrastructure for, 108–10, 161–2
  monitoring system for, 161–2
  new staff for, 162
Tax
  bonded areas, 30
  credits, 26, 30
  havens, 24–5
  income, 27
  losses by China, 26, 149
  minimization of, 21
  on dividends, 28
  on interest, 28–9, 133
  on management fees, 29
  on royalties, 29, 133
  planning, 18–26
  treaties on, 133
  withholding, 25, 28, 30, 133
Thin capitalization, 68
Tianjin, 11, 167
Tibet, 11
Transactional net margin method, 35,
  78
Transfer pricing, 172–3
  and OECD Guidelines, 35
  Chinese practice for, 26
  definition of, 18

in concept, 18–30
international laws, rules and
    regulations for, 51–5
methods, 34–5, 71–8
OECD Guidelines for, 35
regulations in China for, 45–8
tax losses by, 26, 149
Type 'A' form, 102–3
Type 'B' form, 102–3

United Kingdom, 33, 43–4
United States, 17, 33, 178
    transfer pricing rules of, 37–9

Vertically integrated business, 59–60

Wei Jianguo, 170
Western Region, 11
Wholly foreign-owned enterprise, 8, 176
Withholding taxes, 25, 28, 30, 133

Xiamen, 167
Xie Fuzhan, 171
Xinjiang, 11

Zhejiang Province, 171